Building the New Museum

Building the New Museum

Suzanne Stephens, Editor

The annotated proceedings of "Art Against the Wall," a three-part symposium on the architecture of art museums, sponsored by The Architectural League of New York on December 5, 10, and 12, 1985.

Participants

Colin Amery
Edward Larrabee Barnes
Arthur Drexler
Michael Graves
Charles Gwathmey
Hugh Hardy
Malcolm Holzman
Robert Hughes
Philip Johnson
Alex Katz
Rafael Moneo
Norman Pfeiffer
Alan Plattus
Helen Searing
Suzanne Stephens, moderator

The Architectural League of New York
Princeton Architectural Press

Suzanne Stephens, Editor
Anne Rieselbach, Managing Editor
Kate Norment, Copy Editor
Michael Bierut, Vignelli Associates, Designer

This publication was made possible
by a grant from Formica Corporation.

ISBN 0-910413-33-9

Distributed in Great Britain,
Europe, and the British
Commonwealth by The
Architectural Press.

This book was typeset by
Intergraphics, Inc. in
Garamond #3. It was printed
and bound by Eastern Press,
New Haven, CT.

The Architectural League of
New York, 457 Madison Avenue,
New York, New York
10022

Library of Congress Cataloging-in-Publication Data

Building the new museum.

    ''The annotated proceedings of ''Art Against the
wall'', a three-part symposium on the architecture
of the art museums, sponsored by the Architectural
League of New York on December 5, 10, and 12, 1985.''
    1. Art museum architecture—Congresses.
2. Architecture, Modern—20th century—Congresses.
I. Stephens, Suzanne, 1942-   . II. Amery, Colin.
III. Architectural League of New York.
NA6695.B85   1986   727'.7'0904   86-25575
ISBN 0-910413-33-9

Contents

I would like to thank all the participants in the panel discussions, who clearly put a lot of thought and passion into their observations and presentations. We very much appreciate the time and effort certain panelists gave in providing material for the publication. I am sorry that schedule conflicts prevented other architects of recent museums from participating as well.

As moderator of the three panel discussions, I must extend special thanks to Rosalie Genevro, Executive Director of The Architectural League, who helped organize the series of programs and, with her staff, smoothly staged the well-attended occasions.

As the editor of the publication, I would like to extend my deep appreciation to the squad of committed, intelligent, and energetic people who made it possible: managing editor Anne Rieselbach, copy editor Kate Norment, and designer Michael Bierut. I also want to express my appreciation to Rosalie Genevro, whose overall guidance throughout the varied stages of the publication process was indispensable, and to other League employees who appeared at certain critical moments to give their time and invaluable assistance: Christopher Flacke, Alison Zucrow, Christopher Lemelin, and James Reginato. I would particularly like to thank Deborah Kirk, who was brought in as a special consultant to supervise (and perform a good portion of) the grueling task of substantiating for print the many nuggets of information casually spilled forth in the heat of the debate. I must also add that without Dorothy Alexander's masterful photographs taken during the symposium, we would not have been able to truly convey the spirit of the occasion—in all its forms—for this publication.

Suzanne Stephens
Editor

Foreword

With this volume, we introduce a new publication series from The Architectural League of New York.

Our intent is that this series will record lectures and other programs at the League that seem to have a broad significance, and will present original work of particular importance.

We are greatly indebted to Gerald Allen, who has contributed his vision, experience, and professionalism as General Editor of the series, to Ulrich Franzen of the publications committee, and to the Board of Directors of the League for their support in this new endeavor.

We thank Susan Grant Lewin and Formica Corporation for believing in the value of our efforts and generously providing the funding that has made possible this first volume.

We are grateful to Lily Auchincloss, whose support helped make possible the programs on which this publication is based.

Suzanne Stephens originated the idea for "Art Against the Wall: Building the New Museum," which was presented as a symposium in New York in December 1985. She directed and moderated the panels most effectively and has now shaped this publication so that the ideas and information first presented during those evenings can reach a wider audience.

Frances Halsband
President, The Architectural League of New York

Introduction
Suzanne Stephens

In this series of evening discussions sponsored by The Architectural League, we will investigate the issues involved in the planning and design of a number of new art museums. In the first evening we will analyze and debate features of old and new museums in order to isolate their peculiarities, their strengths and weaknesses. During the subsequent two evenings we will scrutinize the current work of seven architects who have been approaching museum design in separate and distinct ways. From the presentations, discussions, and analysis that take place in these three sessions, we hope to arrive at an understanding of the special factors that influence museum architecture today, and possibly to discern a direction that future museum design should take. The issues we plan to address involve not only the museum's design, but also its urban and civic presence, its cultural role in society, and its symbolic significance.

This debate is occasioned primarily by the proliferation of new museums for art, some of which are substantial extensions of existing museums. Major museums have recently opened in Portland (Maine), Los Angeles, Miami, Atlanta, Fort Lauderdale, Richmond, and Des Moines, not to mention England, France, Germany, Italy, and Japan.

We are confining our discussion to art museums alone because they so aptly embody the cultural values and attitudes prevalent in postindustrial societies today. The contemporary art museum is a product of the economic forces that affect the creation, buying, selling, and viewing of art in the late twentieth century. The proliferation of museums in the 1980s in the United States, Europe, and Japan is closely linked not only to the health of these countries' economies, but more particularly to the international art market, itself buoyed by the increasing value of art as a commodity.[1] In the United States, for example, art collectors are encouraged by tax laws to donate art to museums and to help pay for the extra gallery space—the new wing, the new building—needed to house the art they have donated. If tax laws encourage such munificence, civic pride further inspires it. Particularly in the growing cities of America's Sunbelt, the construction or expansion of a museum has become an expeditious means for establishing a cultural presence.[2] Large corporations, as well as city and state governments, see the advantage of supporting new museums: their largesse helps shape an identity for the area, which in turn reflects well on the patron.

But the art-museum boom also owes much to the growing audience for art, which writer Mark Lilla has argued derives from the United States' program for higher education in the post–World War II years. He suggests that a "new-brow" cultural class has been formed midway between the "high-brow" and "middle-brow" classes that Russell Lynes outlined in 1950.[3] This stratum of culturally voracious new brows desires

8

and responds to the museums' increasingly didactic exhibitions, with their extensive wall labels, accompanying acoustiguides, and strongly educational organization. I would also conjecture that this cultural appetite is linked to the technical nature of higher education. While educated people are confident of their training in professional and technical areas, they may feel quite deficient in the knowledge of traditionally accepted arts and humanities, yet know enough to feel embarrassed of their ignorance.

With the increased popularity of museums, there are more people to contend with. More equipment is needed, more guards, more curators, more management staff to keep things running. Bigger budgets are required to pay for all of this, and the need for income is met, often, with more shops, restaurants, and other commercial amenities that generate revenue as well as serve the public. Museum shops alone constitute a significant enterprise: while shop sales totaled $35 million in 1979, that figure increased in the last few years to about $200 million annually.[4]

Until recently it seemed that the museum had replaced the church as the institution central to our cultural and social life.[5] The identity and image of the museum is changing, for it now doubles as a community center, a school, a shopping center, and often a movie house. And increasingly—now that large fundraising dinners and gala parties at museums are becoming commonplace—the museum functions as an unusual sort of country club. Faced with the program for a new museum, the architect has to take these changes into consideration, trying to design spaces that respond gracefully to so many types of activities.

In looking at the changing demands and pressures put on museums, we should first ask what a museum is meant to do for the art it contains. For many people, the museum is the place to go simply for the discovery and contemplation of art. In stating the basic goals of a museum, philosopher Nelson Goodman in his book *Of Mind and Other Matters* has put it exceedingly well:
The museum has to function as an institution for the prevention and cure of blindness in order to make works work. And making works work is the museum's major mission.... Works work when by stimulating inquisitive looking, sharpening perception, raising visual intelligence, widening perspectives, bringing out new connections and contrasts, and marking off neglected significant kinds, they participate in the organization and reorganization of experience and thus in the making and remaking of our worlds....Even the most able work, however, does not always work. Whether it does...will depend also upon the capacities and condition of the viewer, and the surroundings and circumstances of the viewing.[6]

In examining the means by which museums currently attempt to make "works work," we can see a range of architectural responses, some more successful than others. As a formal and programmatic building type,

the museum belongs to a tradition distinct from other forms of architecture. Nonetheless, the museum has often borrowed its architectural imagery from other types of structures—such as palaces and houses for the museum of the nineteenth century, factories and warehouses for the museum of the early twentieth century, or even sculptural forms for the museum of the post–World War II era. And today, the question of what the museum should look like is still not settled. Equally at issue are questions of the planning and design of the gallery spaces themselves: What kind of installation and lighting methods foster communication between the viewer and the art object? What sort of balance should be maintained between the architecture and the works on display? How should the museum respond to the issue of growth and expansion so that it doesn't risk becoming less a museum than a collection of services needed to support the museum? Finally, there is the question of the museum's image. What should the museum represent to the public, and what role should architecture play in creating that image? How should the building respond to the community and, more specifically, to the surrounding physical context? Architecture too often misses the opportunity to modulate and shape these types of communication—between the viewer and the object, between the museum and the community. But now we should begin our analysis.

9

Notes

1.
See Grace Glueck, "The Art Boom Sets Off a Museum Building Spree," *New York Times,* 23 June 1985, sec. 2, p. 1. As Glueck notes, there is now a "growth in art facilities across the country that makes the building spree of the 1970s, once thought to be abated, look like a practice run." Glueck cites a number of reasons for the growth, including the good press art has received, which arouses public interest, and the high prices art attracts, which appeal to a consumer-oriented society. Artists have also contributed to the situation, since many of them are very prolific, producing a good deal of work, much of it requiring new, bigger buildings.

2.
Ibid. Glueck attributes the growth of new museums partly to demographic shifts: Fort Lauderdale, Florida, for example, has become more culturally competitive as it has gradually changed from a resort town to a city of affluent year-round residents, while the success of the high-tech industry in San Jose, California, has prompted that city's quest for an arts facility.

3.
See Mark Lilla, "Art and Anxiety: The Writing on the Museum Wall," *The Public Interest* 66 (Winter 1982), pp. 37–54, in which he discusses the influence of postwar higher education on young professionals—the "new brows." He explains, "The new brows are...forever trying to bring middle brow up (public television) or high brow down (Mostly Mozart festivals)." Lilla emphasizes that this group formulates its cultural tastes according to education, not income or social class. Viewing art no longer has to do with contemplation, he says, but has become an event, tightly shaped and directed into a didactic experience.

4.
The 1979 figures are from the Museum Program Survey 1979, cited in Lilla, "Art and Anxiety," p. 50. Shop sales for 1985 are estimated. See Barbara Rudolph, "Mixing Class and Cash," *Time,* 9 December 1985, p. 56.

5.
See Mark Lilla, "The Great Museum Muddle," *The New Republic,* 8 April 1985, pp. 25–30. Lilla argues that while the American art museum has become popularly accepted, its position as a social institution is unclear. Although he does not consider the museum to be "at the center of American civic life, as are our most important government buildings," it has stood for the culture's common aspirations since its conception in nineteenth-century America: "Not devoted to private or shared public consumption, the museum was to be a *symbol* of the importance a city's citizens placed on art." The museum's moral role, says Lilla, was established early on by the institutions' philanthropist-founders, who believed in the arts' positive effect on the soul.

6.
Nelson Goodman, "The End of the Museum?," address to the Association of American Museums, in *Of Mind and Other Matters* (Cambridge: Harvard University Press, 1984), pp. 179–81.

Colin Amery
Architecture critic for the
Financial Times, *London; an*
advisor to the National Gallery
search committee to select an
architect for the gallery extension.

Robert Hughes
Art critic for Time. *Hughes*
writes frequently on art for the
New York Review of Books
and other publications.

Philip Johnson
Partner in the New York firm
John Burgee Architects with Philip
Johnson. Johnson has designed
fifteen museums in his
architectural career.

Alex Katz
Painter. His work was the sub-
ject of a comprehensive survey in
March 1986 at the Whitney
Museum of American Art and has
frequently been exhibited at such
museums as the Museum of Mod-
ern Art in New York and the
High Museum of Art in Atlanta.

Helen Searing
Professor of art history at Smith
College, curator of the exhibition
"New American Art Museums,"
mounted at the Whitney Museum
of American Art in 1982, and
author of the accompanying
catalogue of the same name.

Suzanne Stephens
(Moderator)
Architectural writer, editor, and
commentator. She has written
numerous articles on museums.

Art and Architecture

An overview and discussion of past and present
museums
December 5, 1985

The Development of a Museum Typology
Helen Searing

Selecting an Architect
for the National Gallery Extension
Colin Amery

Discussion
Colin Amery
Robert Hughes
Philip Johnson
Alex Katz
Helen Searing
Suzanne Stephens, moderator

The Development of a Museum Typology
Helen Searing

I conceive as my task tonight, in the time allotted me, to show you as many images of museum design as possible. My commentary, therefore, will be brief and perhaps outrageously general, but we can address more specific issues after the slide presentation.[1]

You should also bear in mind that I have a particular prejudice or preference regarding museum design, which I should confess at the outset: the most successful museum designs are those that in some way—however tentative, however attenuated—reach back to the architectural tradition of the public museum as it evolved as a building type in the late eighteenth and early nineteenth centuries. Even when the type is modified to suit the needs of the individual institution and transformed to reflect contemporary realities of economics or technology, its functional and formal value remains.

Thus I find troubling the modernist rejection of typology in favor of a universal solution, based on advanced technology, for all museum programs. Early examples of this jettisoning of museum typology were the schemes prepared for the Museum of Modern Art in 1930–31 by George Howe and William Lescaze. In their design, which resembles a commercial structure or a series of maisonettes, there is no specific imagery that says "museum" to the viewer. This attitude reached its apogee in Mies van der Rohe's work, especially the New National Gallery, built in Berlin in 1962–68. Here Mies' preoccupation with universal space, the glazed pavilion, and an extremely refined steel structure has been applied to the program of the art museum. In such an articulated flowing space, the curator for each exhibition must also act as architect; the fact that all of the exterior walls of the main floor are of glass makes it even more difficult to hang pictures. The permanent collection, housed in the basement floor formed by the podium, receives little natural light.[2]

One could argue, of course, that the first public art museums, that is, the first buildings in which collections were opened to the general public, were not specifically designed for that purpose but were fitted into houses or, more properly, palaces. Nevertheless, within the house or palace particular rooms were developed to suit the display of art. In the seventeenth-century Grande Galerie of the Louvre, for instance, long narrow halls were found to be ideal for the purpose of the temporary exhibition of work emanating from the Royal Academy. When Napoleon opened the Royal Collections to the public in 1793, the Grande Galerie became the centerpiece of the future Musée du Louvre. Some of our favorite museums, such as the Frick Collection in New York City and the Phillips Collection in Washington, D.C., were initially inserted into or added onto houses. But in building a new museum, it is useful to keep in mind the typology developed specifically for the art museum during the

1
Project for the Museum of Modern Art, New York. Howe and Lescaze, Scheme four, second variation, 1930.
2
Project for the Museum of Modern Art. Scheme six, 1931.
3
New National Gallery, Berlin. Ludwig Mies van der Rohe, 1962–68.
4
New National Gallery.

5

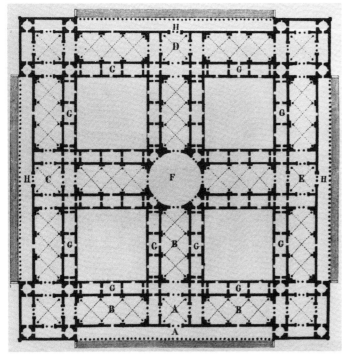

age of Enlightenment, when it became one of the constituent institutions of the city. Particularly in France architects were concerned with developing a solution that would address the possibilities and problems involved in the exhibition, protection, and conservation of works of art.

In 1802–05 the French theorist J.-N.-L. Durand published a paradigmatic design for a museum consisting of a series of long galleries, in this case vaulted, that surrounded four courtyards and a rotunda. The spatial formats and structural prototypes codified by Durand recur in museum design throughout the nineteenth century. The beauty of Durand's monumental proposal was that one did not have to follow the entire project, which in its vast scale was typical of late eighteenth-century idealized architecture. Portions of it could provide inspiration, as was the case with Leo von Klenze's Glyptothek in Munich, designed in 1816: four vaulted wings enclose a single central courtyard that provides light through windows to the interior, but the exterior walls are unfenestrated for maximum security. Von Klenze provided a sympathetic environment for the antique sculpture that makes up the contents of the Glyptothek, and he heightened the traditionally educational mission of the museum by making the building itself a collection of the different vaulting types encountered in antique architecture. Barrel vaults, shallow domes on pendentives, and pantheonic rotundas with skylights have been fitted inside a shell that suggests a Greek temple penetrated by low unbroken wings.

The long gallery was considered the ideal space for viewing art in the Dulwich College Picture Gallery, built outside London in 1811–14 and designed by Sir John Soane. It offers a sequence of variable-length spaces illuminated from above by an innovative system of monitor lighting. Light enters through clerestory windows set in the vault rather than directly through a skylight, and the intensity of the sun's rays is thereby tempered. The Dulwich Gallery is also an early example of a museum that incorporates other functions, and thus is prophetic of a number of late twentieth-century museums. It was intended to include an almshouse for old-age pensioners, and does in fact contain the mausoleum of the museum's donor. The mausoleum forms the frontispiece of the building, and its function is signalled by the sarcophagi and funeral urns that decorate, in Soane's typically idiosyncratic manner, the projecting wing.

Like Durand's paradigm, the Glyptothek and the Dulwich Gallery are one story in height, but museums quickly increased to two-story heights. Karl Friedrich Schinkel's Altes Museum in Berlin, of 1823–30, rises a full two stories above a monumental base. Rather than marking the entrance with a temple front, Schinkel stretched a great stoalike colonnade across the main facade and introduced what would become another

16

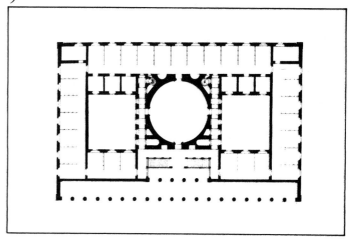

5.
Project for a Museum. J.-N.-L.
Durand, 1803.
6.
Glyptothek, Munich. Leo von
Klenze, 1816–30.
7.
Glyptothek.
8.
Altes Museum, Berlin. Karl
Friedrich Schinkel, 1823–30.
9.
Altes Museum. Plan of upper
floor.
10.
Dulwich College Picture Gallery,
London. Sir John Soane,
1811–14.
11.
Dulwich College Picture Gallery.

popular feature in museum design: the grand stair. Like von Klenze, Schinkel utilized portions of Durand's museum project, as shown by the Altes Museum's central rotunda and inner courtyards. The rotunda, along with the ground-floor galleries, was used for the exhibition of sculpture; on the second story, Schinkel increased available display area by adding panels set perpendicular to the outer walls. Additionally, through the use of generous windows on these outside walls, Schinkel not only provided additional surfaces for paintings but allowed them to be bathed in natural light. Another early museum, the Museo Pio-Clementino in the Vatican of the 1770s, offers yet again the motifs of the rotunda and the monumental stair.

The Durandesque typology of museum design prevailed until the mid-twentieth century, as the National Gallery in Washington (today, the West Wing), designed by John Russell Pope and opened in 1941, confirms. And although in many ways it is a resonantly iconoclastic work of architecture, the Guggenheim Museum, designed by Frank Lloyd Wright over the years between 1943 and 1959, suggests that he too was reaching back to the rotunda tradition when he conceived the great central top-lit space. Furthermore, the profile of the spaces where one simultaneously circulates and views works of art resembles that of Durand's galleries—but in the Guggenheim the galleries continuously unfold rather than being set parallel or perpendicular to each other.

Meanwhile, an alternate tradition evolved that would affect museum design and offer a radically different paradigm: the building type initiated by the great expositions, the earliest example being the Crystal Palace in London, constructed in 1850–51. These huge *machines à exposer* were built for the display of objects, particularly manufactured goods, but also provided for the temporary exhibition of works of art. This tradition has been revived in the second half of the twentieth century through the creation of museums that function as transparent containers with vast, relatively open and amorphous spaces. The museum as exposition hall can be seen in the Centre Pompidou in Paris, by Piano and Rogers, which opened in 1977, and in the recent additions of Roche/Dinkeloo to the Metropolitan Museum of Art. The skin of these additions is entirely of glass; it encloses large open spaces that require architectural interventions within the envelope to make the spatial volumes suitable for museum purposes. Also necessary are devices to block the light. (One could put Mies' New National Gallery in this group as well.)

It was probably inevitable that Louis Kahn would be the architect responsible for directing museum design back to its early typology. Obsessed with the role of natural light in defining architectural form and making architectural space palpable, Kahn studied the effect of light not only on the surfaces of buildings but on works of art themselves. Further, Kahn was very con-

13

14

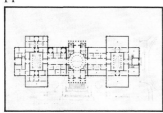

15

16

12.
National Gallery of Art, Washington, D.C. John Russell Pope, 1937–41.
13.
National Gallery of Art.
14.
National Gallery of Art. Plan of main floor.
15.
Altes Museum.
16.
Solomon R. Guggenheim Museum, New York. Frank Lloyd Wright, 1943–59.

17.
*Crystal Palace, London. Joseph
Paxton, 1850–51.*
18.
Crystal Palace.
19.
*Centre Georges Pompidou, Paris.
Studio Piano and Rogers,
1971–77.*
20.
*Metropolitan Museum of Art,
New York, Temple of Dendur in
the Sackler Wing. Kevin Roche
John Dinkeloo and Associates,
1978.*

21.
Kimbell Art Museum, Fort Worth, Texas. Louis I. Kahn, 1969–72.
22.
Kimbell Art Museum.

23.
Yale Center for British Art, New Haven, Connecticut. Louis I. Kahn, 1969–77.
24.
Portland Museum of Art, Charles Shipman Payson Building, Portland, Maine. I. M. Pei & Partners, Architects and Planners, Henry N. Cobb, Design Principal, 1978–83.
25.
Portland Museum of Art.

cerned with identifying the specific nature of individual institutions and expressing that nature through the ordering of the plan. In the Kimbell Art Museum in Fort Worth, of 1966–72, Kahn returned to the ideal of the vaulted gallery, examples of which we have already seen in the work of Durand and his followers. But, seeking greater flexibility than was possible with the load-bearing masonry walls of nineteenth-century buildings, Kahn brought together the modern desire for the concept of flowing, interpenetrating space with an emphasis on clarity and order, which he imposes and reinforces by the rhythm of the structural system of his museum. In the Kimbell Kahn was able to provide spaces that are roomlike, with a sense of enclosure like that provided by traditional galleries, but that can easily be rearranged and opened up when necessary. Filtered natural light spills down the inner shell of the vaults and tempers the artificial subsidiary illumination. Natural light also enters the galleries from the side, through windows that open onto courtyards which, as was typical of earlier museums, contain sculpture.

At the Yale Center for British Art in New Haven, of 1969–77, Kahn pursues a similar strategy of providing flexibility while simultaneously rejecting the totally fluid space of modernist museums. Again one encounters that characteristically sympathetic interplay between the structure of the building and the spatial sequences: while the square module provides a sequence of underlying order, with its repetitive pattern marked on the floor, the concrete skeleton allows for a variety of gallery sizes. Rather than relying on the long barrel vaults seen at the Kimbell, at the Yale Center Kahn uses a series of square domical vaults, each capped by a skylight. He includes two interior courtyards, one of which is at the entrance and extends the full height of the building. It is topped by a clear skylight, although those over the galleries are fitted with filters.

Both the Kimbell and the Yale Center have had a tremendous influence on subsequent museum design. In the Charles Shipman Payson Building of the Portland (Maine) Museum of Art, designed by Henry Cobb of I.M. Pei & Partners and completed in 1983, certain features from the Kahn museums are probed and reinterpreted. I believe that Cobb himself would be the first to acknowledge the impact of the Yale Center in his utilization of a geometric order that structures the space, in the sequence of rooms of differing heights, and in the use of natural light streaming down from above, carefully controlled so that it does not harm the works of art. The longitudinal sweep of the top-floor galleries recalls the Kimbell, but the emphatic patterning of the floor through granite paving with inset pine boards stresses the square module that underlies the plan. The Portland Museum also attempts to refer back to an older institution—the Dulwich Gallery—for light penetrates not directly through a horizontal skylight, as in the Yale Center, but through domed, louvered clerestories.

However much the interiors of the Yale Center and the Portland Museum address directly the issue of how a museum is experienced, the exteriors of each are institutional. In the Portland Museum the exterior is determined by the downtown context. Through design elements such as the loggia on the ground floor and the Kahn-like circles at the top of the main facade that, according to Cobb, "engage the sky," the architect has tried to instill some of the majesty associated with museums, but the result is mixed at best. The Yale Center, with its group of shops lining the Chapel Street facade, was probably the first museum to incorporate commercial space, a precedent that other museums are following to gain extra revenue. Kahn's use of stainless-steel panels to enclose the spans between the carefully detailed concrete skeleton is perhaps sufficiently striking and unusual to endow the austere exterior with a mystery and novelty appropriate to a university museum.

Another museum addition that follows Kahn's method for top lighting galleries is that designed for the J. B. Speed Museum, in Louisville, Kentucky, by Geddes Brecher Qualls Cunningham: Architects, completed in 1983. Here one encounters long vaulted galleries and smaller rooms that bring together the organizing systems of the Kimbell and the Yale Center.

Kahn recreated a museum tradition for the late twentieth century by employing new structural systems while restoring old planning types. More recently some contemporary architects have looked not to Kahn's example so much as directly to the early nineteenth century (as Kahn himself did). The Neue Staatsgalerie in Stuttgart by James Stirling and Michael Wilford, of 1977–84, obviously refers to Schinkel's Altes Museum in the organization of the exhibition galleries around a great rotunda on the second floor. Of course, Stirling must comment on the Schinkel model in a way that speaks to his time, so there is a kind of fragmentation in the new work that distinguishes it from the old. Thus Schinkel's columned facade, which contains the mass of the building, has disappeared in favor of a series of volumes that project and recede along the street. The rotunda, while still used for the display of sculpture, is missing its dome, and the vegetation springing up and over its stone walls suggests that the museum has become a romantic ruin. This, as well as the pieces of masonry that have apparently "fallen" out of the wall to either side of the main entrance, is a design decision that could seem to question the very nature of the museum enterprise. Modern fragmentation or schizophrenia is also suggested by the clash of brightly painted high-tech materials with surfaces faced in local stone.

26.
J. B. Speed Art Museum, Louisville, Kentucky, South Wing. Geddes Brecher Qualls Cunningham: Architects, 1983.
27.
Neue Staatsgalerie, Stuttgart, upper floor gallery. James Stirling Michael Wilford and Associates, 1977–84.
28.
Neue Staatsgalerie.
29.
Neue Staatsgalerie.

In contrast to the fluid spaces of the main floor, the exhibition areas on the second floor are organized as a suite of rooms. As in the Altes Museum, they surround the rotunda on three sides and form an enfilade of

30

31

32

33

34

30.
High Museum of Art, Atlanta, atrium. Richard Meier and Partners, 1980–83.
31.
Anchorage Historical and Fine Arts Museum, Anchorage, Alaska. Mitchell/Giurgola Architects, 1984.
32.
Hood Museum of Art, Dartmouth College, Hanover, New Hampshire. Charles Moore and Chad Floyd, Centerbrook Architects, 1981–85.
33.
Hood Museum of Art. Upper floor.
34.
Hood Museum of Art.

galleries without a separate circulation route. Top lighting supplements the side illumination of Schinkel's museum and is successfully augmented with artificial light. On the interior, too, the theme of fragmentation is apparent, especially in the pieces of molding that are wrenched from their logical context to "decorate" the galleries.

Except for some of the high-tech materials and the ramps that circle the rotunda and provide passage from the lower street at the front to the higher one at the rear, the Neue Staatsgalerie in Stuttgart would seem to have nothing in common with the High Museum of Art in Atlanta, by Richard Meier, completed in 1983. Yet the delicate renderings prepared by Meier for the High force us to remember Schinkel. In the crisply beautiful pen-and-ink drawings, the technique for delineating the trees is derived from the German master, as are some of the figures. Further, within the heart of the High, the memory of the rotunda remains. Whereas Stirling removed the dome and exposed the rotunda, Meier has trimmed it down to a quadrant—modern incompleteness versus preindustrial wholeness. Another reference, to the Guggenheim and its ramps, surfaces as well. Meier has restricted the ramp's purpose to circulation, rather than combining movement and viewing as at the Guggenheim, but the same opportunity to gaze across the central space to see works of art from a distance operates here.

I would like to conclude with a brief overview of certain motifs that are very much in favor among museum designers at this moment. In the recently completed Anchorage Historical and Fine Arts Museum in Alaska, by the firm of Mitchell/Giurgola, in addition to the top-lit central space suggestive of the traditional rotunda there is a dramatic stair meant to elevate the museum experience. Such a grand stair appears as well in Stirling's Sackler Museum at Harvard, the addition to the Fogg Art Museum that opened in the fall of 1985. In Hans Hollein's Municipal Museum Abteiberg in Mönchengladbach, of 1972–82, a series of variously configured stairs separates the different rooms and stimulates the museumgoer to be aware of the architecture no less than of the works of art. The Dallas Museum of Art by Edward Larrabee Barnes Associates, of 1983, provides a monumental cantilevered stair that leads from the main circulation space to the second-floor galleries. In Dartmouth College's recently completed Hood Museum of Art in Hanover, New Hampshire, by Charles Moore and Centerbrook Architects, a grand stair similarly leads one from the entrance up into a soaring, top-lit space containing contemporary art. The stair itself, clinging to the main facade, is rather constricted, and there is a wonderful sense of release as one enters the generously scaled top gallery, enhanced by the brilliantly colored paintings hung there. In contrast to the symmetrically placed and centered stairs of the older museums, those cited above are placed at the side.

The return to the use of natural light in museums, especially light introduced from above, and to the creation of specific rooms, rather than unarticulated universal spaces, to establish a firmer sense of containment for the works of art has been demonstrated in examples described earlier.

An issue that I haven't dealt with directly but that I understand the panelists may address later is that of the urban context of the new museum or museum addition. In Cobb's building in Portland and in Stirling's Sackler, an attempt is made to relate the building to its surroundings through the color and texture of the materials. In Portland locally produced water-struck brick was used in combination with granite to blend the museum addition into its environment, but the scale remains somewhat overpowering in relation to its neighboring structures. In Cambridge Stirling was not able to use the brick he originally specified. The red and black brick he finally decided on perhaps makes a gesture to the polychromed Victorian Gothic–style Memorial Hall nearby, but it makes no more concession to the materials of the original Fogg Museum than does the detailing. And until the proposed bridge to that building is constructed, the design of the facade has no rationale.

While some of the materials of Stirling's building in Stuttgart are sympathetic to the nineteenth-century museum to which it is appended, the sleek texture and vivid pop-art colors of the high-tech elements, as well as the sloping walls of glass, seem at odds with traditional masonry architecture. In terms of context, probably the most successful recent design is that of the Hood Museum. Its architects were faced with the problem of mediating between the 1950s bulk of Hopkins Center [designed by Harrison & Abramovitz] and the Romanesque Revival Wilson Hall. As Paul Goldberger astutely observed on the occasion of the formal opening of the Hood in the autumn of 1985, Moore and his associates have performed the miracle of making two older buildings look better than they did before, bringing equilibrium and harmony to the complex at last.

There have been many interesting solutions to museum design since the mid-twentieth century, though perhaps we still have a way to go before we see the balance and successful functioning, in both pragmatic and expressive terms, shown in the Altes Museum. Not only did the Schinkel building provide a hospitable home for works of art, but the architect also took note of the surrounding city and established this portion of Berlin as a precinct for the arts.

35.
Arthur M. Sackler Museum, Harvard University, Cambridge, Massachusetts, entrance. James Stirling Michael Wilford and Associates, 1979–85.
36.
Arthur M. Sackler Museum. Main stair.
37.
Arthur M. Sackler Museum. Third floor gallery.
38.
Municipal Museum Abteiberg Mönchengladbach, West Germany, upper level gallery, garden wing. Hans Hollein, 1982.
39.
Municipal Museum Abteiberg Mönchengladbach. Axonometric.

Selecting an Architect for the National Gallery Extension
Colin Amery

All I can say is, "Come back, Karl Friedrich Schinkel." After having had such an instructive and useful general survey of new museums, I want you just for a moment to bear with me in considering a very specific problem. If you would, imagine yourself in Trafalgar Square with your back to Nelson's Column and Whitehall. You're standing in the square planned by John Nash. His job was not unlike Schinkel's: he had to impose a certain order and classical shape to the center of London. The National Gallery grew on that site in Trafalgar Square, and its facade is roughly the same as it was when it opened in April 1838. The architect, as you know, was William Wilkins, who designed the National Gallery at the tail end of the Greek Neoclassical revival. The Museum did not open to universal acclaim.

One of the questions we might consider this evening is whether we need so many new galleries and museums. At the time the National Gallery was first discussed, the English landscape artist John Constable had very strong views about whether it was needed. He wrote a letter to the impending trustees in 1822: "Should there be a National Gallery, which is talked of, there will be an end of the art in poor old England, and she will become, in all that relates to painting, as much a non-entity as every other country that has one. The reason is plain. The manufacturers of pictures are then made the criterion of perfection instead of nature."[3] Constable had a point.

If you look at museum architecture at the end of the eighteenth century and the beginning of the nineteenth, you can see as rapid a growth then as now. The opening of the Public Art Gallery in Vienna in 1792 was followed very quickly by others in Paris, Munich, Madrid, Berlin—all in a period of about forty years. We're really into another wave of museum expansion, now that new museum construction is occurring in a number of countries.

The site of the new extension to the National Gallery, which used to be occupied by a furniture depository that was bombed in World War II, was bought by the government in 1958. It's a very difficult site in many ways, since it's a crucial piece of London townscape. And the new building will have to try to make something of Wilkins' design. With the Hood Museum, Charles Moore seems to have improved the bad buildings next door. In some ways, that's what's needed in Trafalgar Square.

The new extension is for a very specific purpose: to house the pre-Renaissance pictures, of which the National Gallery has one of the finest collections. We're trying to house some of the greatest pictures in the world, such as Piero della Francesca's *The Baptism of Christ*. At the moment it's in a very uncomfortable position, surrounded by too many other pictures, and it's hard to see. Masaccio's *The Virgin and Child* is one

24

40.
National Gallery, London.
William Wilkins, 1832–38.

of the most marvelous pictures in the collection. It has a great sense of foreboding, not only in the context of the scene depicted, in which the Virgin looks with a troubled face at her rather miserable child, but also in terms of the artistic signs the picture presents that herald the arrival of Renaissance art. The work came from the Church of the Carmine at Pisa and has always been a public picture. It's been in the National Gallery collection for nearly seventy-five years, and it needs a new room. Jan van Eyck's *The Arnolfini Marriage* is a more private picture; the viewer, for the first time perhaps, is looking into someone else's completely private world. That imposes tremendous demands on the kind of room this picture should be seen in.

One opportunity we will have for the first time in the new National Gallery building is to hang together pictures from north and south of the Alps that were painted around the same time. There is a large northern European collection of German and Flemish pictures, including Memlinc's *The Virgin and Child with Saints and Donors ("The Donne Triptych")*. At the moment this complete altarpiece is badly displayed in an overcrowded gallery, and there has been some attempt to place fake altars under some of the other pictures, which is very unsatisfactory. What we hope will come out of the new design is a way for viewers, as they walk through the collection, to perceive the artistic links between north and south Europe. By seeing all these pictures in the right conditions and in

41.
Jan van Eyck, The Marriage of
Giovanni Arnolfini (?) and
Giovanna Cenami (?) ("The
Arnolfini Marriage").
42.
Masaccio, The Virgin and
Child.
43.
Hans Memlinc, The Virgin and
Child with Saints and Donors
("The Donne Triptych").

sympathetic surroundings, lit in a certain way, we may
better understand the artistic climate of pre-Renaissance
Europe.

This is what the architect has to bear in mind—we
want the kind of place where you can respond most
effectively to pictures of this quality. When we were
looking at the short list of candidates to build the new
wing, one of the things we wanted to discover from the
prospective architects—and I think we succeeded in
finding this out—was how they react to pictures, and
how they want us to react to the museum's pictures
when they're hanging in their new setting. After all,
that's the most important thing.

In the National Gallery the ordinary classical rooms are
reasonably good for looking at pictures. They are
top-lit and they're very simple. These rooms are perfectly all right. They have one or two features that
might be improved, but there's nothing major to
object to about them. It's the treatment of these rooms
by the curators that has been lamentable, to say the
least. The early Renaissance paintings are often surrounded by unpleasant hessian (burlap) walls; ugly
numbering over the doorways; ill-conceived furniture,
usually out of scale with the pictures; unattractive
finishes on the floors. The general dowdiness of the
settings makes you think that perhaps the curators only
see the pictures, not what is around them. There have
been one or two attempts to introduce rather more
fashionable elements of museum display—that is, the
incorporation of contemporary furniture and objects into
the galleries—but the curators forgot to take out some
of the other objects. Why put in antique objects and
furnishings to make the place seem more like a room
and leave the hideous furniture that has been put in
since the 1960s? So, many of the problems in viewing
pictures don't have to do with the architecture, but
with curatorial considerations. This extends not only to
the conservation and treatment of works, but also to a
certain contempt for the people who look at pictures,
an attitude common in even the newest museums. The
National Gallery had nearly three million visitors last
year. These rooms are extremely crowded nearly every
day of the year.

As for the architecture itself, it's generally thought
that you have to surround pictures with some kind of
architectural tour de force. In one perfectly good classical gallery, where Dutch pictures were rehung around
1969–70, the works were thought to be too small for
the gallery. So the gallery was made to fit the pictures.
You now have to climb up small stairs to a platform,
as though you were going up into a nursery to peer at
the pictures. The other fate this room has suffered is
having egg-crate ceilings installed—a phenomenon, I
think, not entirely confined to the United
Kingdom—in order to lower the ceilings and make the
place more "human." The result, of course, is that you

26

have neither architecture nor art, and the pictures are hardly helped by this kind of treatment.

In our search for an architect to solve these problems, we looked at new museums in America and Europe. Members of the search committee got excited every time they went into a new building and were pulled immediately toward the pictures. That's the kind of building we're looking for. It's quite a rarity, although we did find it in some American museums.

We want the client to play a major role, but we don't entirely believe that the competition process is the right way to do this. So we've gone in for a kind of compromise, with a short list selected from a long short list. The short list, we hope, will produce not a final design but an approach to a design, although, of course, we also want to see what the architects are going to do. For the short list we've chosen two American architects—Robert Venturi, and Henry Cobb of I. M. Pei & Partners—and the rest British architects—James Stirling; Piers Gough; Jeremy Dixon, a youngish architect who at the moment is extending the Royal Opera House in Covent Garden; and Colquhoun & Miller, a firm known in the States because Alan Colquhoun teaches at Princeton. This firm extended the Whitechapel Art Gallery, converting an Arts and Crafts building into a modern gallery.

When museum directors at the Seattle Art Museum were proposing the limited competition for that museum, Robert Venturi wrote them, explaining in great detail why he wouldn't enter the competition. He had a good point: he said that he always preferred to buy a ready-made suit because he knew what he was getting. The museum changed its tack—to interviews—and Venturi won. The dilemma for those proposing an architectural competition is, how much do we want the architects to design before we commission them to build the building?

There are certain things we definitely want in this building. We want a response to art. We want a sympathetic environment for the public. We want proper rooms, not these things called "roomlike rooms"; what is a roomlike room if it's not a room? We want character. We want permanence. We want a quality of finish. We want a kind of dignity in the building. We want a variety of room sizes. We want good lighting, which is problematic because curators are practically paranoid about light. It's all very well for Louis Kahn to have said that light shapes the building, but it's interesting that every single picture at the Kimbell is spot-lit, artificially lit. There is wonderful light for the building itself, but the pictures have to be lit artificially. We do want the kind of luminosity Kahn was talking about, but we want it to directly affect the pictures. This I think is the problem: how to bring together the art of architecture and the art of art, which are perhaps not quite the same thing.

44

45

44, 45.
National Gallery.
Views of galleries.

Discussion

Colin Amery
Robert Hughes
Philip Johnson
Alex Katz
Helen Searing
Suzanne Stephens, Moderator

Moderator (Suzanne Stephens): In a lecture he gave at the Fogg Art Museum in 1984, Philip Johnson brought up several issues about the nature of seeing art in a museum.[4] Philip, would you elaborate on some of those points?

Philip Johnson: I think building a museum is a lot simpler than it's been made out to be. What makes it difficult is that museums are also public monuments; they have taken the place of churches and palaces. But looking at pictures is quite easy, and museum architecture should be a matter of arranging spaces for seeing art. This was done well by Stirling and by Schinkel. If you just follow their example, you'll be all right in hanging pictures. Hang them in a simple room, and create an enfilade of rooms so you know which way you are going. The sense of orientation is absolutely essential. Also, in terms of what the building looks like, you want what used to be called in the old days "monumentality." You can't use the word anymore, but the desire for that quality is still there. You don't want to go into the Museum of Modern Art [renovated and expanded by Cesar Pelli and Associates], which is just a loft building parading as a work of architecture. You want to go into a Michael Graves building, maybe, where you have a wonderful piece of architecture. But then after you get in, you want to be in the Stuttgart or Berlin museums.

Moderator: At Harvard you said that with regard to an enfilade of rooms, one should have at most five in a row. Stringing many more together would destroy the sense of orientation and procession.

Johnson: And then there is the problem of getting in and out. It's all part of the processional experience. You have a terrible time in Stuttgart before you get up to see the rooms—you've got to go up a ramp. Schinkel's entrance, with stairs, was much better. I think perhaps we should leave out Stirling and just let Schinkel "talk."

Moderator: You also said the sense of containment that you get in a room is very necessary.

Johnson: A room is a room is a room. That's why I like what Colin Amery just said—that the National Gallery addition had better have rooms, where you can see pictures and know where you are. That modern architecture thing—with movable partitions—is gone. We're over that, over, over. We're back to where Schinkel put us. Let's stay there.

Moderator: Robert, you have written a lot about museums; in fact, you wrote in a very complimentary way about the loftlike spaces at the Museum of Modern Art.[5]

Robert Hughes: Yes, I must say I rather like those loftlike spaces, but I don't like the frames around the

28

pictures. I think the new framing tends to make all the pictures look like pedagogical exercises in the history of art rather than works that should be seen for their own quality.

Moderator: We're also talking about the room as a frame. Would you elaborate on what you discussed about how the lighting and the clarity in the Museum of Modern Art make the paintings really stand out? For example, you said about the Matisse room: "Its matchless Matisses now constitute one of the great museum rooms of the Western world."[6]

Hughes: The gallery in the Modern where the Matisse works are installed works very well indeed because it provides adequate light for the paintings. Because of a long band of glass, it has natural light. I'm afraid a lot of museum lighting tends to isolate the unfortunate masterpiece like a rabbit caught in the glare of a halogen lamp on the road at night.

Moderator: As a matter of fact, the Museum of Modern Art tends to do that, too. There are very few rooms that have natural light.

Hughes: That's true. The reason I singled out the Matisse room is that it's a particularly successful one. Matisse was, as we know, obsessed with natural light and the attempt to create equivalents for it in the degree of abstraction he was using. In the case of the gallery at the Modern, the balance between the internal light of the Matisse paintings and the external light coming into the room works very well. But the lighting in other rooms of the museum is not so successful.

The thing I like about the Modern—although I don't think of it as being by any means a perfect job—is that some of the spaces are aedicular. They provide a pleasant shift of scale that brings you into some kind of intimacy with the work of art. But then, being an art critic, I can see the works under privileged conditions, when the museum is empty. One problem for the museum designer is that the small rooms can get clogged with visitors and the artworks become invisible behind the human screen. This certainly happens in the Modern when it's very full. One of the great museum pleasures is being in the Uffizi when it's empty. But trying to see *Primavera* through a screen of thirty-five pairs of armpits is not what Botticelli intended.

Moderator: Alex, since you have exhibited your work in many museums, I wonder if you have any thoughts on what kind of spaces are best for viewing your art?

Alex Katz: You need to consider museums in terms of the appropriateness of the space for the art that's being shown there. In the British Museum or the National Gallery, spaces can be designed to suit the collections. In a contemporary-art museum, the situation is more open-ended.

46.
Left to right: Helen Searing, Philip Johnson, Alex Katz, Robert Hughes.
47.
Museum of Modern Art, New York, renovation and addition. Cesar Pelli and Associates, 1984. Gallery showing works from the museum's Matisse collection.

The room I liked best was one in the Jewish Museum before the ceiling was lowered. It was a beautifully proportioned room and had a lot of stability. As I recall, it measured about 40 by 60 feet and didn't have doorways breaking into the middle of the walls: it had openings at the ends of the long walls, so the short and long walls were relatively unbroken. When a room is half the size of the Jewish Museum room, say 20 by 30 feet, and the doorways are placed in the middle of the walls, then there are really no walls at all.

The lobby I like best is Frank Lloyd Wright's Guggenheim Museum lobby. When you go in from the outside world, you're immediately in a sensational space with a lot of art. As for the galleries within the Guggenheim, they have paintings on one side and an atrium on the other, creating spaces that are inadequate for contemporary painting. Similar situations exist at the Los Angeles County Museum of Art and the Art Institute of Chicago. The Guggenheim seems to function well for medium-size and small paintings and for colorful sculpture, but it's absolutely no good for large paintings. I couldn't show there because my paintings are too large and I like a contained space. The Museum of Contemporary Art in Los Angeles is a space I'd love to show in.

Johnson: The old one or the new one?

Katz: The Temporary Contemporary, designed by Frank Gehry. It's just a plain factory, with walls you can put wherever you want. It has high ceilings, beautiful proportions, and very nice light. When looking at contemporary painting, there are certain spaces you feel great in and others you don't. If the space is too large, the paintings become postage stamps; if the space is too tight, you can't see them. The Temporary Contemporary seems to be a space that fits contemporary paintings very well. There is a big difference in scale between modern and contemporary painting. Most of the museums we've been looking at have not dealt with the scale of contemporary painting at all.

To return to lobbies, I think the Metropolitan Museum lobby [renovated by Roche/Dinkeloo] is just awful. I don't see any reason for that horizontal entry space. The Museum of Modern Art's lobby, another horizontal entry space, is unsatisfying, too. I want to see art when I go to a museum. I don't want to see an information desk or benches or a lot of books.

Moderator: Do you want to see architecture?

Katz: That's secondary to me, although I do get an architectural rush going into the Guggenheim, which deals with the entry so elegantly. It's a real piece of architecture. Philip Johnson's Sheldon Art Gallery in Nebraska is also a real piece of art. It has a great space, with a beautifully proportioned lobby.

49

50

48.
Alex Katz.
49.
Installation view of the Alex Katz exhibition at the Whitney Museum of American Art (March 13-June 15, 1986).
Left to right: One Flight Up, 1968, *and* The Blue Umbrella #2, 1972.
50.
Sheldon Memorial Art Gallery, University of Nebraska, Lincoln, Nebraska. Philip Johnson, Architect, 1963.

Johnson: It goes vertically and not horizontally.

Katz: Yes. The ones that go horizontally are pretty awful.

It takes three or four people to make a bad museum situation. It takes a curator, a trustee, an architect, and, at least in contemporary shows, an artist. A good example of a bad museum situation is the Rijksmuseum Vincent van Gogh in Amsterdam [designed by Rietveld, van Dillen & van Tricht], where there are intimate paintings hung in a very large room with low ceilings. The museum does handle traffic well—you can walk anywhere you want—but nothing looks good. The paintings are lit with fluorescent lights, and they're framed in imitation nineteenth-century frames.

Hughes: Since we're citing our "faves" in bad museums I would certainly like to suggest the Centre Pompidou. This is *the* archetype and supreme example of everything that a museum should not be, beginning with the curious idea of the transparent and modular museum that can adapt to various kinds of functions—a chameleon-like space that can embrace whatever happens to settle in it. To make things worse, this must be the world's only all-steel-and-glass building in which there is literally no natural light at all because of the mass of ducts, registers, pipes, conduits, and other impediments on the outside of the building. It's an amazing contradiction in terms. On top of that, the French seem incapable of keeping it clean or even minimally maintained. What you end up with is this extraordinarily compromised solution—not a solution at all—of dragging Gae Aulenti over from the Musée d'Orsay in order to put up opaque walls inside the famous transparent museum of the future.

Moderator: The Beaubourg curators said they needed the more permanent enclosed space on the fourth floor, designed by Gae Aulenti, since the art from 1905 to 1960 was of a smaller scale than the art executed since 1960. Dominique Bozo, director of the Musée National d'Art Moderne, decided to separate the space into smaller-scale and more permanent rooms. He kept flexible, open-ended partitioning elsewhere where he thought it was applicable for today.[7]

Katz: I think Beaubourg's a mess. Flexible space works sometimes—at the Temporary Contemporary it's absolutely sensational. Most of the artists I know love that space. For exhibition rooms in New York City, the best are on the fifth floor of the Brooklyn Museum, where there are a series of generous spaces (one about 40 by 60 feet) and galleries with skylights. You go through the galleries in the middle of the room as in most older museums, which is not ideal, but I do think they're the best rooms. The fourth floor at the Whitney Museum is the most versatile space in the city right now. But I think the lack of decent spaces in New York City for seeing contemporary painting is awful.

Hughes: Most contemporary painters have tended to squeeze themselves out of that market. A lot of the time the problem we're talking about is not so much a matter of the artwork's scale in relation to the human body or the room, but simply a matter of the artwork's brute size. I'm talking about large, inflated works of art. You can't necessarily hang everything of that size.

The Museum of Modern Art was conceived in a world where a very large painting was about five by five feet. With the exception of certain Matisses and some of the larger Picassos and so forth, classical early modernist pictures are generally about two feet by three feet—about the size of a Cézanne or a Miró. Although I completely agree with Alex Katz about the beauty of the spaces at the Brooklyn Museum, the problem is that museums are confronted with art never envisioned at the time they were built. This is the problem with the Guggenheim. The Guggenheim is one of the most hostile spaces imaginable for showing contemporary painting. This is due in large part to Frank Lloyd Wright's contempt for arts other than his own and that of the Japanese print. You can't hang large pictures, which establish strong horizontal axes, on a floor sloping at an angle of four degrees without it looking as though there's something hideously wrong in the hanging. And although people say it's nice to look across the Guggenheim and see other pictures at a distance, you actually can't do that because the bottoms are often cut off by the inclined parapet. The effect is rather like that in the High Museum.

Moderator: What is your impression of the High Museum? How does that parti work? The galleries there are not on a slant—they are separate from the atrium and ramps.

Hughes: My feeling is one of disappointment in the work of an architect I very much admire and like in principle. You walk in and think, "What a terrific building!" Of course, your initial impression of the building may be jarred somewhat by the utter mediocrity of the collection.

Moderator: Except for the furniture collection, for which Richard Meier also designed the installation.

Hughes: Yes, the furniture installations and the installations of small objects are very sumptuous, but they remind me of a remark supposedly made by Queen Mary when she was taken around the reinstallation of the Victoria and Albert Museum. The objects in the V & A had been brought out of their aboriginal clutter and displayed in vitrines, isolated for solitary contemplation. This, I remind you, was very rare in museology in the thirties and forties. Anyway, after being taken through this installation by the assembled bigwigs, the Queen was asked for her impression. She is said to have replied, "Wonderful, charming." Long pause. "Such a pity, don't you think, that everything

31

51

52

51.
The Saatchi Collection, London.
Max Gordon Associates, 1985.
52.
Museum of Modern Art. Es-
calator bank leading to design
galleries.
53.
Helen Searing.
54.
Philip Johnson.

53

54

looks as though it's for sale?"

As art fans, art consumers, art critics, and what have you, we've gotten used to a system of presenting works of art that verges on the Tiffanyesque. We are in fact subliminally being sold things as the rudiments of paradise and the very bricks of immortality. Museums overdesign their installations. Stuart Silver's installation designs in the Metropolitan have been a classic example of this, and so is Richard Meier's work in the High Museum. There's just too much of the vitrines. There are beautiful objects in them, and some very interesting ones. But there's a curious choppiness to the High Museum. You're constantly looking through square openings in partitions at half-visible paintings. You just want a plain white wall with a masterpiece hanging on it.

Amery: They don't have any masterpieces.

Hughes: No, they don't. But then it would be better to have a plain wall.

Moderator: Philip, you're in the beginning stages of designing a museum for the Los Angeles County Museum of Art.[8]

Johnson: Schinkel.

Moderator: So it's going to have rooms—five rooms—with a grand entrance.

Johnson: Alex Katz is going to design the size of the rooms. They're going to be around a court, so the side light will give some relief. There won't be many windows looking into the court, but you do have to have some recognition of the outside. There will also be top-lit galleries and a grand staircase, because I like grand staircases. I don't want ramps. Otherwise, it will be a very simple building.

Moderator: The windows looking outside are to break up...

Johnson: The experience of being in a basement all the time.

Moderator: You designed an underground museum for yourself in New Canaan that I believe has no windows.

Johnson: No windows, but it works just fine because it's so small it doesn't count as a museum.

Moderator: You wouldn't use it as a model for something?

Johnson: A museum should look like...

Hughes: A museum.

32

Johnson: Like Schinkel.

Moderator: Colin Amery brought up the Kimbell, which everybody uses as the paradigm of top-lit, softly lit spaces. But he said incandescent spotlights are still needed for the paintings. Helen, do you think there is a problem in having both?[9]

Searing: The point is to have the capabilities provided by incandescent light but to remove its coldness by mixing it with natural light. All of the top-lit spaces now have incandescent and natural light.

Moderator: At Mönchengladbach Hans Hollein very bravely combines fluorescent light with incandescent and natural light.

Amery: All of which leads to a terrible headache.

Katz: The Saatchi Collection in London does that. It's really terrific.[10]

Hughes: The architect Max Gordon did an extremely good job there. What the issue of natural versus artificial light comes down to, at least in terms of the etiquette of the museum—the method of display or deception—is that a work of art shouldn't have an exterior theater imposed upon it. A work of art shouldn't be treated as anything except an experience which, in its plenitude or its lack of it, is self-sufficient.

There is a tendency to present work in a way that tries subliminally to punch up your experience of it. Architects can either discourage or encourage this tendency, although often they neither completely give into nor completely get rid of it. In those dark, strongly lit chambers below the East Wing of the National Gallery in Washington, which everybody loves except me, there was a show of art and sculpture of the Pacific Islands. By the time the installation designers were finished lighting that show and coming to terms with the basic given of the black cellar rather than the basic given of the Schinkelesque white room, going through the installation was like going into Trader Vic's.[11]

Moderator: In getting back to natural versus artificial light, a lot of curators believe you have to use artificial light for the paintings so that you don't destroy them.

Hughes: Yes, you have to correct with artificial light. Also, of course, a lot of paintings were painted under artificial light. This is not true of Chardin, but it certainly is of a great deal of painting since 1960. The standard lighting in the studio is no longer north light.

Moderator: However, one of your criticisms of the temporary-exhibition galleries in the East Wing is that they do not have a sense of natural light or orientation to the outdoors.

Hughes: It's not just the orientation. This kind of artificially lit space delivers the pictures over to theatricality, and that's what I object to. You don't have to have a window with a view to the outside. It's nice if you can, but it's not essential. You can have top lighting. You can have clerestories.

Moderator: Colin, in finding an architect for the National Gallery in London, are you worried about getting too much "architecture"?

Amery: We desperately want to try to avoid a kind of Bloomingdale's, consumer-oriented approach. How do you like being delivered by escalator to look at pictures? And how do you like having to walk through a shopping center to look at pictures?

Hughes: It's maddening, that sort of thing.

Moderator: You went crazy over the escalators in your review on the Museum of Modern Art in *Time*.[12]

Hughes: I guess it's sort of nice being taken up them—it was sort of like that people tube at Beaubourg. At least the Museum of Modern Art cleans its glass, so it isn't covered with pigeon droppings.

Moderator: What is wrong with escalators? A lot of museums are adopting them.

Amery: It's too much like being in a shopping mall.

Searing: It's the association.

Katz: I think the escalator on the outside of the Beaubourg is terrific.

Moderator: As long as it's kept on the outside.

Hughes: As long as you're looking towards Paris.

Katz: I think escalators on the inside of buildings are not so attractive or nice. There should be a better way of dealing with people.

Moderator: In terms of the balance between art and architecture, do you feel the problem is in hiring an architect who does not obey the program enough? Louis Kahn said, "I believe the architect's first act is to take the program that comes to him and change it. Architecture is a thoughtful way of making spaces. It is not filling prescriptions as clients want them filled."[13] What do you think of that assessment?

Amery: Well, it's okay coming from Kahn, isn't it? I'd just be worried if it came from any of the architects on the National Gallery's short list.

Moderator: One last topic we should address is the continuing growth and expansion of museums.

33

Museums seem to be constantly adding on and adding on and adding on. Do you think the original goals and intents are getting lost? Is there a danger in all this adding on to a museum, which means more money, more curators, more maintenance, and higher budgets?

Hughes: Sure, there's a danger in it. The danger is one of boredom. Museums can become too encyclopedic. They can have too much in them, thereby either wearying their public or producing insoluble difficulties of storage. But the trouble, in this country particularly, is the tax structure that encourages bequests to museums. As shown by the amount of competition for artistic recognition that exists between various cities, the museum replaced the church as the sort of center of civic libido in this country sometime after 1945.

It's very easy to keep on constructing museums ad infinitum, because although there is not a limitless supply of old art, there is a limitless supply of art being made. But old or new, art's natural direction of movement, due to the tax laws, is towards the museum. The museum supplies the suction that constantly drags works of art out of the private sphere into the public—to the advantage of both. So the time must inevitably come when all the works of art made in America or owned by Americans must gravitate towards the museum. We're confronted with a situation that is extremely difficult for any museumgoer to break down or to make sense of.

56

The competitiveness between museums strikes me as unrealistic and foolish. It results in essentially theatrical display. I think it would be much better if, say, Philippe de Montebello [director of the Metropolitan Museum] and J. Carter Brown [director of the National Gallery] could put on gloves and fight it out in the ring once a year rather than constantly inflicting upon us these factitious masterpieces and treasure chests.

Amery: They'd never be able to agree which museum to do it in.

Katz: I think the Metropolitan ought to be decentralized. It would be much better for the city if works of art were spread all over rather than being concentrated in one place. The Metropolitan has about seven or eight museums in one spot, and it would be better if one of them were, say, on 34th Street. The Guggenheim is a finite space and seems perfectly okay. The expansion program at the Whitney is something I think would be wonderfully beneficial for the public. The Whitney has a wonderful collection in storage and it's not being shown, and they could use a more exciting exhibition space.

Moderator: Philip, you've come out for the Whitney's proposed expansion.[14] Do you think the museum's growth is adequately reasoned? Do you think the museum should be that large?

Johnson: I was talking about the architecture. It's beautiful. The program is the business of the museum itself.

Hughes: The Whitney needs space, but I don't think the proposed design is very beautiful. The outside of the building, as far as one can judge from drawings, models, and photographs of models, which is not really adequate, has the delicacy of Albert Speer combined with the color of *Miami Vice*.

Katz: That's not bad.

Moderator: I actually meant the program, though.

Hughes: The Whitney manifestly needs more space. You can't have a museum functioning at its peak capacity if 80 percent or more of its work is in permanent storage with nowhere for it to be shown.

Moderator: It's not really in our purview to get into the issue of how museums should grow or when they should stop growing. It seems that usually museums grow and then, having grown, look at other museums and say, "Okay, now it's time to stop" or "Let's have small museums." Museums might go in the direction of small specialized museums or of miniature Metropolitan Museums, which offer a little bit of something to everybody. But these and other issues we can continue discussing on the next two evenings.

Notes

1.
For an overview of the history of museum design, see Helen Searing, *New American Art Museums* (New York: Whitney Museum of American Art, in association with University of California Press, Berkeley and Los Angeles, 1982). In the book, published to accompany an exhibition of the same name, Searing also provides a synoptic history of the art museum in nineteenth-century America, a discussion of the late nineteenth-century museum explosion, and an analysis of the developments in American museum typology.

2.
This design for an art museum is based on earlier projects for other building types by Mies. The Bacardi Office Building project for Santiago, Cuba (1957–58) is often cited as a prototype for the Berlin museum; and Mies' court house projects of the 1930s certainly explored similar themes. Mies' first built museum was the Cullinan Wing of the Museum of Fine Arts in Houston (1954–58). For more details on Mies' thinking behind these and other projects, including the Museum for a Small City of 1942, see Franz Schulze, *Mies van der Rohe: A Critical Biography* (Chicago: University of Chicago Press, 1985), pp. 230–31, 300–304.

3.
See Michael Levy, *A Brief History of the National Gallery* (London: Pitkin Publications, n.d.).

4.
On 18 October 1984, Philip Johnson spoke at Harvard's Fogg Art Museum in a series of lectures by a variety of speakers titled "Architecture: Mother of the Arts." In his talk Johnson argued that above all clarity is needed in a museum, for with clarity comes a sense of orientation. Clarity is found in traditional museums in which galleries are arranged in a line and in which rooms have visible corners, thus fostering a sense of containment and orientation. Of the historical examples of museums in which a sense of procession, clarity, and orientation is present Johnson pointed to Karl Friedrich Schinkel's Altes Museum in Berlin, Leo von Klenze's Glyptothek in Munich, and John Soane's Dulwich College Picture Gallery outside London. He said that such museums as the Centre Pompidou at Place Beaubourg in Paris by Piano and Rogers or the New National Gallery in Berlin by Mies van der Rohe pose terrible problems for installation. As other negative examples Johnson cited the Metropolitan Museum's new André Meyer galleries by Kevin Roche John Dinkeloo and Associates and the new galleries of the Museum of Modern Art by Cesar Pelli & Associates, all of which lack a sense of sequence or orientation. While Frank Lloyd Wright's Guggenheim Museum does not provide containment in an enfilade of gallery rooms, Johnson said, it does have a "wonderful sense of reference" due to the atrium.

5.
Robert Hughes, "Revelation on 53rd Street," *Time*, 14 May 1984, pp. 78–80. In this review Hughes writes: "Dividends have been wrung from Pelli's calm style. The new MOMA does not creak with intrusive imagery. It does not look like an airport, a temple, a constructivist factory, a tomb or a fortress, to cite the five most popular types of recent museum....The galleries themselves are neutral, not Architecture with an A." He adds: "One of the strengths of the old MOMA was its feeling of intimacy....There was none of the architectural muscle flexing that is conventionally meant to prepare its audience for a Major Experience. MOMA...staff...put a very high priority on preserving this feeling in the new structure" (p. 79).

6.
Ibid., p. 79.

7.
See "Redesign of Galleries, Centre Georges Pompidou, Paris," *The Architectural Review*, November 1985, pp. 86–90, for more details on Gae Aulenti's renovation of the fourth floor of the museum.

8.
The Los Angeles County Museum of Art is considering developing two acres of a site directly across the street from its current facility being expanded by Hardy Holzman Pfeiffer Associates. At this point plans include a 21-story office building with a parking garage, restaurants, shops, and a sculpture garden. Additional museum galleries are reportedly part of a future expansion. A developer has not yet been selected, and schematic designs of the current proposal by John Burgee Architects with Philip Johnson were not released for publication.

9.
The Kimbell Art Museum in Fort Worth has skylights running down the center of each of its barrel vaults, which are 100 feet long by 20 feet wide. Lighting designer Richard Kelly solved the problem of filtering daylight by mounting cycloid-shaped reflectors under the slot in the barrel vault. The reflectors are made of perforated metal, allowing daylight to bounce up against the underside of the curved vault. Spotlights mounted on the edges of the reflectors supplement the ambient light. For more details about this solution and the lighting Kelly designed for the Yale Center for British Art in New Haven, see a profile of Kelly, "Lighting Starts with Daylight," *Progressive Architecture*, September 1973, pp. 82–85.

10.
At 98A Boundary Road in London the English architect Max Gordon designed a small gallery primarily for temporary exhibitions of work from the Saatchi Contemporary Art Collection. The gallery, which is open to the public, is lit by skylights. Natural light filtered through a protective plastic film mixes with fluorescent light that is bounced upward out of metal troughs placed in the roof structure.

11.
For a recent assessment of the East Wing's galleries, see Andrea Oppenheimer Dean, "The National East: An Evaluation," *Architecture* 73 (October 1984), pp. 74–79, in which the author notes that the permanent and temporary galleries have been criticized for the absence of "airiness and natural light." She finds that "the sharp contrast between the atrium's soaring, wide open, light-filled spaces and the artificially illuminated galleries that seem all the more cavelike because of their hexagonal shapes requires a mental shift from fifth to first gear" (p. 78). J. Carter Brown, the director of the National Gallery, told Dean he would like to have more natural illumination for the galleries.

12.
Hughes, "Revelation on 53rd Street." Hughes compares the escalator bank in the Modern's lobby to that of the Centre Pompidou: "But whereas the Pompidou's tube is a mere people mover, MOMA's moving staircases work in a celebratory space, full of light and air" (p. 78).

13.
Quoted in Barbara Weiss, "American Museums: Three Examples," *Lotus International* 35 (1982), p. 103.

14.
At a presentation given on 25 July 1985 to the members of the New York Chapter of the American Institute of Architects and the interested public, Philip Johnson read a testimonial of support by Brendan Gill, a member of the Whitney's building committee, and admitted to "admiring the building enormously."

Edward Larrabee Barnes
Architect with a practice in New York. His firm has designed a number of museums, including the Walker Art Center in Minneapolis and the Scaife Gallery at the Carnegie Museum of Art in Pittsburgh.

Arthur Drexler
Director of the Department of Architecture and Design at the Museum of Modern Art in New York.

Hugh Hardy
Architect and principal of the New York firm Hardy Holzman Pfeiffer Associates, which has designed or renovated museums such as the Cooper-Hewitt Museum (the Smithsonian Institution's National Museum of Design) in New York and the Brooklyn Children's Museum.

Malcolm Holzman
Architect and principal of Hardy Holzman Pfeiffer Associates.

Norman Pfeiffer
Architect and principal of Hardy Holzman Pfeiffer Associates.

Art and the Walls Within

Issues of installation, circulation, and lighting in recent museums
December 10, 1985

Currier Gallery of Art
Hugh Hardy

Virginia Museum of Fine Arts
Malcolm Holzman

Los Angeles County Museum of Art
Norman Pfeiffer

Dallas Museum of Art
Museum of Art, Fort Lauderdale
Edward Larrabee Barnes

Response
Arthur Drexler

Discussion
Suzanne Stephens, moderator

The Currier Gallery of Art
Hugh Hardy

The Currier Gallery is a project of particular interest to me because it represents an investigation of two common themes: continuity and context. If one looks closely at Manchester, New Hampshire, it emerges as a place quite unlike any other. Because this project is an addition to a much-loved building, we believed it should represent a modulation, not a transformation, of the institution it houses. The results are a continuation of an architectural tradition, but invigorated by a contemporary sensibility.

The Merrimack River gave rise to Manchester. The water power it provided, as well as a large immigrant population and enlightened entrepreneurs, produced a major city. The community life of this company town centered around its mills, which can be clearly seen in the brick buildings by the river. The buildings' solidity, strength, and self-assurance celebrate the people who built them, and speak of a benign policy toward labor. In the downtown area the original aristocratic leadership of this city built the kind of handsome civic buildings evident in many New England streetscapes. But this urban fabric is, alas, being transformed by indifferent, packaged bulks, built to honor a different set of cultural values.

Moody Currier was a politician and a man of sufficient means to leave his property to Manchester to establish a novelty: the city's first museum of art. This gift completely stunned everybody in the community. No one knew he had cared about art. And even though he left the resources to create such an institution, Currier had no collection, only an idea. The museum was located in a residential neighborhood, once connected to downtown by streetcar. The Currier was constructed from designs by Edward Tilton, also the architect of the Manchester Public Library. But the original architect for this building was the firm of Carrère and Hastings, the most stylish architects of their day next to McKim, Mead and White. They were in their Spanish-American period and produced a wonderfully fanciful design for the building. The people of New Hampshire thought it absurd. They didn't want Mediterranean architecture in New England. For ten years nothing happened with the project. Five years later, Edward Tilton was hired. He had come into prominence by winning the competition for Ellis Island, and his work for the Public Library was highly esteemed in Manchester.[1] Although the building Tilton designed for the Currier has much in common with the Renaissance palazzi of Italy, it is not a pure example of this style because it is also tangled up with the Beaux-Arts. It is not a three-dimensional sculptural object in the way many Italian buildings are. Instead it is characteristic of the period (1929) in its use of very flat surfaces.

The Currier has always been appealing in its intimacy and personableness. Unlike buildings created to impress the viewer with their size and magnificence, the Currier, with its small scale, simple plans, and

40

1.
Currier Gallery of Art, Manchester, New Hampshire. Tilton and Githens, Architects, 1929.
2.
Currier Gallery of Art addition. Hardy Holzman Pfeiffer Associates, 1982.

The Currier Gallery of Art
Manchester, New Hampshire
Architect: Hardy Holzman Pfeiffer Associates; Hugh Hardy, partner-in-charge; Kurt Kucsma, associate; Maurice Farinas and Sergio Zori, project architects.
Program: A major extension to a regional art museum, including 5,000 square feet of gallery space and 10,000 square feet of support space.
Structure and materials: Beige brick facing on steel frame.
Cost: $2 million.
Consultants: Stanley H. Goldstein, structural; R. G. Vanderweil Engineers, Inc., mechanical and electrical; Jules Fisher & Paul Marantz, Inc., lighting; Peter George Associates, Inc., acoustical.

41

landscaped setting, permits the whole to be easily understood in a single visit. This is an institution in harmony with its residential setting. We have intentionally tried to retain this alliance between a public building and its private neighbors.

A limited competition was held to select the architect of the Currier's addition. We suggested that the rear elevation was incomplete and offered the best location for expansion. Rather than merely extending the existing rectangular volume, we proposed adding two symmetrical pavilions, which would be connected by a new circulation route along a colonnade. A major new entrance to the north would give wheeled access on grade to the gallery's central entrance hall. Together the pavilions and the north entry would form a new entrance court level with the first floor of the old building. Our plan was accepted, and as a result the neighboring street was closed and an extension was built to the north on adjacent land owned by the gallery. This approach offered a remarkable series of options: a special exhibition could be set up in one gallery while changing exhibitions could be placed in the other; both pavilions could be opened to connect with existing galleries; a new exhibition could be installed while the permanent collection remained open to visitors.

The organization and scale of the interiors in the extension are patterned after those in the existing building. The Currier's shaded setting allowed us to filter natural light through skylights and windows to an extent some professionals would find disturbing; no natural light whatsoever seems to be the norm. Generous skylights are used in our addition, but these are translucent, not transparent. Many artists find the new interiors particularly agreeable for the display of work because of the changing quality of natural light from one time of day to another.

We also attempted to solve the bugaboo of how to arrange movable partitions. Because the Currier's budget does not permit reconstruction of entire new rooms for each exhibition, we decided on very straightforward paneled units. The flexible walls are made of standard panels that can be placed in a variety of patterns. They can also be made into freestanding units. They rest on the floor and are braced with metal rods attached to the trusses above.

How did we decide on a traditional solution for the exterior? Why does it look the way it does? The new spaces could have been created with more contemporary materials—glass-block walls, for instance. The trouble with such a scheme is that you can't see the paintings. Furthermore, such aggression would seem odd in relation to Tilton's gentle building. Although not a first-class piece of architecture, the Currier is well loved by the people who use and support it. Its formal composition of a columned entranceway, a facade, a

3

3.
Currier Gallery of Art addition.
Interior.

42

reflecting pool, and monumental stairs has always symbolized "museum" to the community. It therefore seemed presumptuous to compete with these symbols, to say "Look at me!" We did not wish to close up the existing front door and deny past associations of entry. Instead, both old and new entrances are still used, meeting in a central hall. We sought a way to offer complementary public access, not a total reorientation of the existing building.

We decided to use masonry for the new facade since it would defer best to what was already in place. But to replicate the detail of the original facade would have been an injustice to Mr. Tilton and would have been far too expensive. A literal interpretation of Italian architecture might have taken us to something more vigorous and more three-dimensional than the original Currier design. We had a wonderful time thinking about what this new palazzo might be. We began to look at front doors and how you enter traditional buildings. We even considered more abstract versions of Renaissance vocabulary. We nonetheless saw no reason why the use of masonry inhibited a contemporary solution. Finally, we decided to approximate Tilton's limestone detailing in standard brick, but without any curvilinear profiles. There are a few special sections required for the corners and the columns, but the majority of the facade, even the arch, is made from a basic brick module. This addition is basically a continuation of the architectural principles that organized the original. Although stylistically more abstract on the exterior and technically more contemporary on the interior, it represents a tempered extension of the original. No one could mistake this as the work of Mr. Tilton or be unclear about when it was built. This is a contemporary response to the growth of an institution that has used tradition to reveal the present.

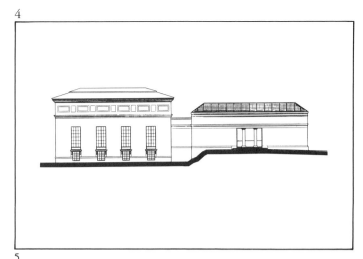

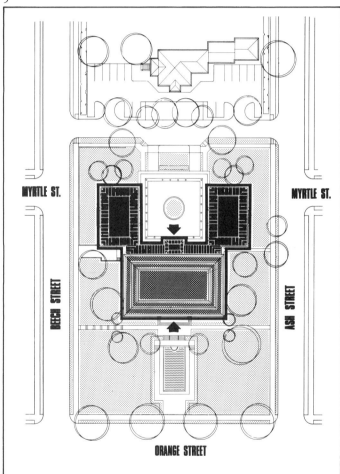

4.
Currier Gallery of Art addition.
East elevation.
5.
Currier Gallery of Art addition.
Site plan.

43

The Virginia Museum of Fine Arts
Malcolm Holzman

Nineteen eighty–six is the fiftieth anniversary of the Virginia Museum of Fine Arts. It was the first visual-arts institution founded and primarily funded by a state, and its employees are, in fact, state employees, although the art it contains has come from private sources. The construction of the new West Wing was spurred by the donation of the wonderful but dissimilar collections of Mr. and Mrs. Paul Mellon and Frances and Sydney Lewis.[2]

We were fortunate in knowing what kind of art would be placed in the building, for the new spaces could be easily tailored to the specific collections. The installations will be semipermanent. Most of the Mellon objects are on display, although small portions will change from time to time. In contrast, the Lewis collection, which amounts to nearly 2,000 objects, will be seen in rotating exhibitions lasting about six months. This collection's range and variety are enormous, both in the content and in the size of the objects. Whereas the Mellon collection is distinguished by small nineteenth-century pieces, the Lewis collection consists of many contemporary objects, as well as decorative-arts objects dating from the middle of the last century to the middle of this century.

One challenge in the design of this building was to realize something high in quality but economical to build. Half the money for construction was provided by the state. The project was publicly bid, and construction work was carefully monitored. In fact, the building cost only $193 a square foot.

The museum was built in four separate stages starting in 1934. The original museum building, designed by Peebles and Ferguson, is a small but somewhat overblown symmetrical Georgian house with simple circulation: from a two-story central space you move out into a ring of galleries.[3] The facade is almost entirely limestone, but you get the feeling that if the architect had had a slightly bigger budget it would have been all limestone. It is very three-dimensional, and while not a glorious building, it is very respectable, with nice detailing. This is true not only of the windows and doors, but also of their enframements and pediments. It is a building that looks terrific in the strong Virginia sunlight.

In the 1950s an addition containing a Mediterranean-style court was built. It extends along the cross axis and the ring of galleries. The exterior uses limestone at the bottom and top of the facade and brick in between. The detailing is considerably flatter than that of the original building. Another wing was added in 1970 that extends the composition to the south, making another interior space called the Renaissance Court with surrounding galleries. Its exterior elevations are plainer. There is almost no limestone; brick dominates. The cornices and beltcourses do not line up with those of the original.

44

6

6.
*Virginia Museum of Fine Arts,
Richmond, Virginia, West Wing
entrance. Hardy Holzman Pfeiffer
Associates, 1985.*

7.
*Virginia Museum of Fine Arts.
Original entrance, east facade.*
8.
*Virginia Museum of Fine Arts.
Exterior, West Wing.*
9.
*Virginia Museum of Fine Arts.
Main space of the Lewis Con-
temporary Galleries, West Wing.*
10.
*Virginia Museum of Fine Arts.
Central hall, West Wing.*
11.
*Virginia Museum of Fine Arts.
Mellon Galleries, West Wing.*

In the 1970s a piece of "modern" architecture was added. The original main entrance was closed; two new entrances placed on the diagonal obscured the museum's basic axial organization. The curvilinear elevations of this addition are made entirely of flat brick surfaces, bordered by a limestone band at the top of the walls and a cantilevered entrance canopy.

The new West Wing is at the back of the existing museum and connects to all four buildings. It also faces a group of historic houses and a chapel located in the six-acre Robert E. Lee Memorial Camp Confederate Park. Yet the actual site for the new wing looked like the back of a strip shopping center: art, supplies, and garbage moved through the same interior corridors to the west facade, and because the museum had been built in so many pieces there was a confusion of service doors, entrances, and fire exits. In addition, mechanical equipment, truck docks, and a security station were randomly located along this neglected elevation.

The design for the West Wing reorganizes these previously unconsidered functional elements. At the same time its architectural expression is intended to acknowledge the presence of the historic buildings in the park. In choosing the exterior material of the West Wing we ignored the vast quantities of brick used in recent additions and returned to the original limestone. We tried to generate the shade and shadow of the original without resorting to classical detailing. We have intentionally created many varieties of limestone textures with crisp detailing. Two glass enclosures on the terrace contain stairwells and patterned ceramic glass that filters out 80 percent of the light. These diagonal interruptions also give a more human scale to the 300-foot-long building. The base of the building is made of rusticated blocks and capped by a great bull-nosed section that forms the top of the terrace. At the very top of the building polished granite bands are made to bump into two existing cornices at both their north and south ends. We built a large-scale mock-up on the site to make sure our contractor, who was bidding in a public and open market, would construct the building the way we wanted. The mock-up also gave us the opportunity to refine our details and to confer on such things as joints, caulking, and the coloring of the building.

After considerable exploration, we decided to base the final interior design on a variation of the original architects' planning intentions, with a central space, surrounding galleries, and intersecting axes directing circulation. The West Wing plan specifically recognizes and incorporates the east-west axes established in the original museum. In spite of its size, the new building does not contain a true front door since the existing structures have three. Instead, the entrance is through circulation routes that lead from the four existing structures into the West Wing and its new public hall. In this public hall are two "view corridors," or

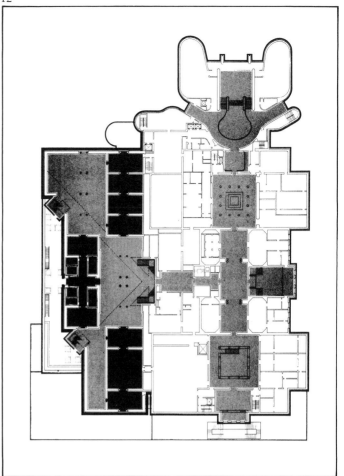

*12.
Virginia Museum of Fine Arts. Plan of main floor, showing West Wing, center left; Lewis Collection, top left; Mellon Collection, bottom left; original (main) entrance, center right.*

West Wing, Virginia Museum of Fine Arts
Richmond, Virginia
Architect: Hardy Holzman Pfeiffer Associates; Malcolm Holzman, partner-in-charge; Neil Dixon, project architect.
Program: A fourth addition to an existing museum, adding 90,000 square feet of exhibition and support space and a new entrance to the museum theater.
Structure and materials: Concrete frame; buff-colored limestone and granite cladding on exterior; Verona marble in main hall.
Cost: $17.4 million.
Consultants: LeMessurier Associates/SCI, structural; Joseph R. Loring & Associates, Inc., mechanical and electrical; Jules Fisher & Paul Marantz, Inc., lighting; Jaffe Acoustics, Inc., acoustical; Ralph V. Ward, Ltd., security.

bridgelike mezzanines, that intersect the longitudinal axis and extend in a V. All circulation routes in this wing now link to earlier parts of the building.

The main hall and its cantilevered stairs leading to the balcony mezzanines are covered with Verona marble, placed with the darkest pieces at the bottom and the lightest pieces at the top. Thus the walls look as if natural light is filtering in from skylights, even when it is not. The stairs and bridges lead to the north to a series of small galleries in the Lewis collection, plus a large, double-height flexible space. On the opposite side of the hall is a series of galleries for the Mellon collection. These galleries are similar in size to the small ones in the Lewis collection but are treated more traditionally in detail and finish to provide balance to the total composition.

The Los Angeles County Museum of Art
Norman Pfeiffer

I was recently told that the Los Angeles County Museum of Art has become the third largest art museum in America. When it first opened in 1965, 26,000 people were members. Today that number has grown to 75,000. About five years ago we were asked to add a wing that would be named after ARCO (Atlantic Richfield Corporation). It was subsequently named for the Chairman of ARCO, Robert O. Anderson. The primary purpose of this building was to house a collection of modern and contemporary paintings and to provide space for changing exhibitions. The original complex, designed by William L. Pereira Associates in 1964, was composed of three separate concrete-frame structures clad in marble mosaic panels suspended between the major columns.[4] Inside, this design theme was extended to the central atrium of the largest building. All the buildings were linked by breezeways, but the solution simply did not work well as a museum.

Mr. Pereira conceived of this project as three pavilions floating in a pool of water set in a park. As it turned out, this park was also the home of the La Brea tar pits, and the fountains around the buildings eventually started bubbling tar. So the entire concept of individual pavilions floating in water had to be supplanted by the idea of three buildings beached on dry land. The design of a new building also had to address the fact that Wilshire Boulevard has become a major thoroughfare, and the museum now finds itself in the middle of a very urban setting instead of the more rural landscape originally imagined.

Because of the buildings' architecture, the public perceived this institution as containing three kinds of activity, each in a separate building. It could not be perceived as a single entity. There was a great deal of confusion about where the front door really was, and once you had made a choice about which building to enter, it was highly unlikely you would come back outside and go into another one. The overall circulation did not encourage such a route.

All the existing buildings needed to be reorganized before the new wing could be designed or even located. The first step was to create a central court that would operate like the large court of the Metropolitan Museum. Here the public can conduct all of its nonmuseum activities—ask questions, hang up coats, check bags, buy things, and so on. Elevators and stairs connecting various spaces in the original three buildings are housed in the central court, which also functions as a place of orientation to the three levels.

The appropriate design of the Anderson building was, of course, our primary goal. But equally important was the creation of a central court and a landscaped setting for the entire museum. The setting was changed from an informal park to a formal composition appropriate to

49

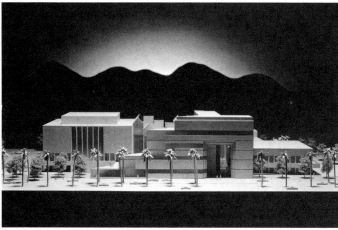

13

Los Angeles County Museum of Art
Los Angeles, California
Architect: Hardy Holzman Pfeiffer Associates; Norman Pfeiffer, partner-in-charge; Stephen Johnson, project manager; Pamela Loeffelman, project architect.
Program: A master plan that includes renovation of 250,000 square feet of existing gallery and support space; programming and planning of a 100,000-square-foot new building for galleries and offices; and creation of a central arrival and orientation point.
Structure and materials: Steel and concrete frame; pink buff Minnesota limestone, terra cotta, and glass block on exterior; porcelain-finished panels in entry and central courts; aluminum curtain wall at entrance.

Cost: $24 million (new building); $16 million (master plan/central court).
Consultants: S. B. Barnes & Associates, structural; Hayakawa Associates, mechanical; Jules Fisher & Paul Marantz, Inc., lighting; Peter George Associates, Inc., acoustical; Hanna/Olin Ltd., landscaping.

the new urban character of this major West Coast cultural institution.

The lower level, which links all buildings, also required replanning. All support spaces are located here. In its depths an unfortunate tangle of art and garbage moved through the same door, and staff and visitors frequently crowded the same corridors. Circulation, security, and conservation standards were all inferior to the norm. Previously curators had been housed in decentralized offices next to their collections. The museum has now opted to bring curators together in one area instead of locating them all over the complex. The lower level of the Anderson building has thus become a newly defined administrative section and an extension of the original lower-level support space.

For the ease of visitors all existing buildings have been reorganized and rebuilt to fit into a long-range development plan. As a result, the new central court and its connecting circulation patterns are now consistent and clear. This sense of orientation was critical to the design. Approximately 100,000 square feet of new construction was needed, a building the size of the Whitney Museum. Fitting a program of such magnitude into the existing complex was one problem; image was another.

What image should this museum convey? This question led to considerable exploration. A similar kind of investigation ensued in the design of the central court. What sort of large hall could orient visitors arriving from Wilshire Boulevard, especially since they would have to move several hundred feet into the central court before actually entering the museum? Finally, we had to ask ourselves what was the appropriate "front door" for this museum, an entity always perceived as three separate pavilions. Ours was the opportunity to create both a symbolic and a very real new presence on Wilshire Boulevard.

The design is based upon the removal of a portion of the programmed volume from the center of the project. It was transferred onto Wilshire Boulevard, thereby creating open space between new and existing buildings. A stairstep configuration was created out of the front facade so that it would not block views of earlier buildings, thus allowing some relation between the new structure and the Pereira buildings. Finally, a multistory gateway was added as the new entrance, and the basic components of the design were in place.

A flexible exhibition gallery for changing exhibitions is located at the plaza level. It contains about 18,000 square feet of virtually unobstructed space that can be organized to suit varying needs. The second public gallery floor has a series of partially fixed partitions that can be used in an open configuration or arranged to create more traditional galleries. The top floor contains a series of regular, small-proportioned "boxes" in which to present smaller, traditional paintings. This uppermost floor has natural light filtered through traditional skylights incorporated in the ceilings.

The central court is an open space covered by a translucent material to allow the diffusion of the dazzling light and sunshine of southern California through all circulation areas. This court also contains a series of bridges and stairs that connect all four galleries. In the future it will also include a grand stairway leading to the second floor.

The exterior of the building is made of three materials: a pinkish limestone, a thin strip of terra cotta, and glass block (used to bring natural light into the galleries). The glass block provides ultraviolet control as well as acting as a sunscreen. An internal louvered shade set within each block diffuses bright sunshine by reflecting it up onto the ceiling. This system gives ambient light to all the galleries along Wilshire Boulevard. The Wilshire entrance is lined with contoured porcelain panels finished with a light pinkish cast.

16
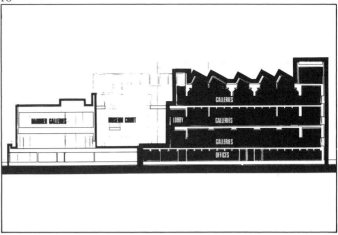

17
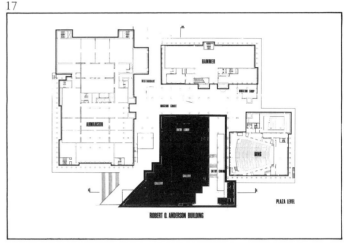

18
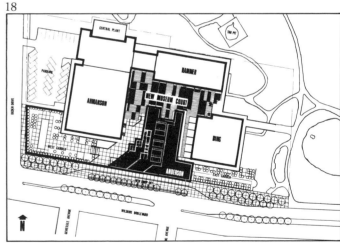

13.
Los Angeles County Museum of Art, Los Angeles, California. William L. Pereira Associates, 1964.
14.
Los Angeles County Museum of Art, model of Robert O. Anderson Building. Hardy Holzman Pfeiffer Associates, 1986.
15.
Los Angeles County Museum of Art. Model of museum court.

16.
Los Angeles County Museum of Art. Transverse section.
17.
Los Angeles County Museum of Art, Robert O. Anderson Building. Plaza level plan.
18.
Los Angeles County Museum of Art. Site plan.

The Fort Lauderdale Museum of Art and the Dallas Museum of Art
Edward Larrabee Barnes

The Fort Lauderdale Museum of Art was sited in a rather depressed downtown area that the Downtown Development Authority wanted to regenerate. Our first plans included a high-rise office tower and a shopping center, all integrated into one design with the museum. As things turned out, the commercial part of the project broke off as a totally separate entity with another architect, and the museum was designed to stand alone. Except for the circulation on the site, there is very little sympathy between the design of our white stucco museum and that of the dark glass office tower in back. The museum nevertheless provides a gateway to the commercial property. An open breeze-way between the auditorium and the museum entrance allows people to walk from Las Olas Boulevard in front of the museum to the shops and parking in back.

The back and sides of the museum are orthogonal to align with the general street pattern. But the front, facing the arc of Las Olas, is designed in sweeping curves, convex and concave. Indeed, the whole composition, inside and out, is a play of convex and concave curves, always set off against the severe rectangular frame of the back of the property.

I have always felt that the problem with the Guggenheim was not so much the curved walls, but the sloping floors and overblown atrium. Some kinds of art, certainly sculpture, look absolutely wonderful against a soft surface where the light is not flat but changing. I like the architecture and art to mesh with each other on an equal basis rather than one being subservient to the other.

The flow through museums is very important, perhaps as important as the actual form. In the Walker Art Center the galleries are arranged around a central elevator core like steps of a spiral staircase. Visitors slowly ascend from gallery to gallery, a few steps at a time, until they come out on the roof, where sculpture is displayed on several more terraces. This circulation was the genesis of the building form.

We designed the Dallas Museum to be an anchor at one end of a new arts district. A tree-lined street runs three blocks from the proposed symphony hall to our museum, which terminates the axis of the street with a fountain court and a great limestone-covered barrel vault. This vault has become the museum's symbol—a monumental gesture proper for a civic center.

Inside this vault is a great curving white space with little architectural detail and continuous reflected light. It is dominated by a huge Oldenburg sculpture and a few large paintings. This is the only monumental space and it is designed to hold art, not to be an empty atrium. The other galleries, most of them 14 feet high, are arranged chronologically on a series of terraces. As at the Walker, one slowly ascends by gentle steps. Each of the terraced spaces has a central shady outdoor

52

The Museum of Art,
Fort Lauderdale, Florida
Architect: Edward Larrabee
Barnes Associates; James
Fraerman, project architect.
Program: A new museum of
64,000 square feet for
irregularly shaped downtown
site.
Structure and materials:
Reinforced concrete frame; rosy
white stucco exterior walls;
terrazzo floors.
Cost: $7.5 million.
Consultants: The Office of
Irwin Cantor, structural; Jack
Green Associates, mechanical.

19.
*Museum of Art, Fort
Lauderdale, Florida. Edward
Larrabee Barnes Associates,
1985.*
20.
*Museum of Art, Fort
Lauderdale. Lobby.*
21.
*Museum of Art, Fort
Lauderdale. First floor gallery.*
22.
*Museum of Art, Fort
Lauderdale. First floor plan,
showing entrance, center; support
services and temporary exhibition
space, right; and auditorium, left.*

23

24

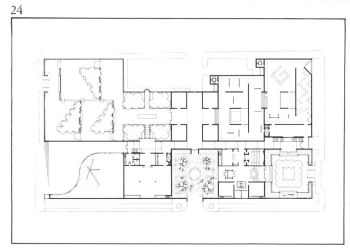

25

23.
Dallas Museum of Art, Dallas, Texas. Edward Larrabee Barnes Associates, 1983. Gallery.
24.
Dallas Museum of Art. Main floor plan, showing Arts District entrance court, middle; linear pedestrian spine, above; Contemporary Gallery, center; art galleries, right; and sculpture garden, left.

25.
Dallas Museum of Art. Contemporary Gallery.
26.
Dallas Museum of Art, showing Arts District entrance.

court and, in two of them, scoop skylights cast day-light indirectly on the surrounding walls. There is great variety—dark spaces, light spaces, boxlike rooms, Miesian screens, all selected to show off the particular pieces and to make the circulation seductive. Again, flow is as important as form.

Dallas Museum of Art
Dallas, Texas
Architect: Edward Larrabee Barnes Associates; Alistair Bevington, principal-in-charge; Daniel Casey, project architect.
Program: A new museum of 195,000 square feet as part of a downtown arts district.
Structure and materials: Steel frame, metal deck, and concrete floors; limestone exterior walls; floors of limestone and oak.
Cost: $29.8 million.

Consultants: Pratt Box Henderson & Partners, consulting architects; Severud-Perrone-Szegezdy-Sturm, structural; Joseph R. Loring & Associates, Inc., mechanical and electrical.

Response
Arthur Drexler

Although the first evening's discussion struck me as somewhat removed from the issue of museum design—for reasons I'll try to go into in a moment—tonight's presentations came to grips with the realities of organizing museum spaces. I thought many of the projects were extremely interesting but also quite problematic. I should mention immediately that I have visited only a few of the museums that were shown tonight. I attended the opening of the Virginia Museum recently, but unfortunately we all arrived so late that we could see the exterior only by moonlight, so I was very glad to see the slides presented here. I have seen the Dallas Museum, but neither the Currier nor the Los Angeles County Museum addition now under construction.

I want to make two general observations. First, almost every one of the museums that we looked at tonight would have a hard time borrowing works from the Metropolitan Museum or the Museum of Modern Art. Do you know why? Too much natural light. The art world is confronting a serious problem today: all art, especially works of the twentieth century, presents enormous conservation headaches. The light levels that are evident in all of the museums we've looked at are increasingly troubling to conservators who are now working around the clock to keep works from disintegrating. This is an immensely costly and time-consuming process. For this reason the easiest way to handle the situation is simply to refuse to make loans, especially of works on paper. Notwithstanding the acquiescence of museum directors and trustees to the proposals of architects, there may be some unpleasant surprises in store in the actual solutions that will affect the programming of these institutions.

The second point I want to make concerns an architectural element that I find very attractive and useful: the glass-roofed space that serves as a garden hall, like the American Wing of New York's Metropolitan Museum and the East Wing of the National Gallery in Washington. In the early sixties, when the Museum of Modern Art was trying to move forward on a very complicated plan for its expansion, one proposal we discussed was the enclosure of the sculpture garden. The idea was that the entire garden could be enclosed in a six-story glass-roofed space with a glass wall and a new entrance on 54th Street.[5] That entrance would have been directly into the garden, which would also have served as the principal circulation system to the various flanking gallery wings. One of the great advantages of this scheme was that the garden would be available on a year-round basis, instead of only two-fifths of the year. The main reason for building such spaces is to facilitate circulation, as is the case with the Los Angeles County Museum, where separate buildings are tied together with an agreeable public space that may or may not absorb the works of art.

56

But a secondary advantage of such large, gardenlike spaces is that they are great entertainment facilities. The existence of museums in a mercantile society has increasingly come to depend on the institutions' ability to lure members, patrons, sponsors, donors, and corporate CEOs to those gala events that make people feel they have arrived in the world. Even though the Met's Temple of Dendur is a third-rate specimen of Egyptian architecture and looks like a paperweight in an airplane hangar, it's a nifty space in which to have dinner. That isn't why it was built, but that's what it's used for.

The cynicism you detect in my comments is genuine, but it also recognizes that the first duty of cultural institutions, as of individuals, is to survive. You can be wrong or you can be right, but if you don't survive it doesn't make any difference. The principal responsibility that museums are now facing is to engineer their own transition in an economic, social, and cultural matrix that is changing very rapidly. Institutions sense that they may be able to guarantee their survival by entertaining the community. That intention now influences the shapes museums are taking. It may not be articulated by the museum administration or recognized by the architect, but it plays a decisive role.

Everybody knows, for instance, that the proposed addition to the Whitney Museum is big, perhaps too big. One of the reasons for its height and size is the administration's determination to have an entertainment facility. If you wish to entertain in a certain way, it is better to do it in a penthouse on the roof than in a basement warren. Most everybody would probably accept the importance of being able to entertain, while rejecting the extra height and bulk it necessitates in this case. It makes little sense unless you know that the penthouse is psychologically a part of the program, so important to the administration of that museum that they're willing to endure the enormous inconvenience and wastefulness of putting a food facility on the roof of a museum. I raise all of this simply to illustrate that architectural solutions are often energized by considerations that no one openly states.

I would like to make one or two additional comments about the individual projects we have been looking at tonight, all of which are enormously interesting. I have a question about the Virginia Museum. The night I visited the museum the great hall of the West Wing was being used as a dining room and was filled with tables, so it was hard to tell what its main purpose was. How is the main hall intended to be used?

Holzman: It's intended to be used like the three similar spaces in each of the existing buildings. You enter these spaces and move to the ones surrounding them. The main hall of the West Wing is where you enter to go to the Lewis and Mellon collections. Six times a year social events will be held in the hall. At some point there might be some large works of art in that space, but not at the present time.

Drexler: That is the answer I assumed you were going to give, to which I would add this observation: the only aspect of the new wing that I was uncertain about was how the main hall would function for any of these purposes—social events or the exhibition of works of art. The galleries themselves are extremely successful and match the exuberance and variety of the two collections. Not only are the galleries different, but the feel of the installations is different too. There is no sense of any of the works being jammed into an arbitrary solution.

I find the Dallas Museum to be a very beautiful and very successful space—a museum that offers a contrast between fixed and square rooms and a more planar Miesian or pseudo-Miesian treatment of space. It's worth remarking that the Miesian open plan was actually developed for residential design and was then applied to exhibition facilities. It was conceived in this museum as a space through which people could move very easily. It is wonderful for the manipulation of traffic, but it also has failings: just as it is easy to move through, it doesn't easily allow people to stop. If you wish to set up situations where people feel they can get out of the flow of traffic, you have to find another solution.

One further problem with the Dallas Museum has to do with the size of recent American pictures. They were generally painted with the assumption that they would eventually be seen in apartments. What this meant was that there was a fixed size on these paintings and that they would be perceived as walls. As a rule of thumb, it's usually true that small pictures tend to look better in smaller-sized rooms. But big pictures do not necessarily look better in very big rooms. Quite often they look best in small rooms where the sheer concentration of space forces the energy of the picture to come at you full blast. This is certainly the case with Jackson Pollock, and it is the case with a number of pictures hanging in Barnes' glorious barrel-vaulted hall in Dallas. Some of these large paintings seem to have shrunk to the size of postage stamps.

Discussion

Edward Larrabee Barnes
Arthur Drexler
Hugh Hardy
Malcolm Holzman
Norman Pfeiffer
Suzanne Stephens, Moderator

Moderator (Suzanne Stephens): Let's take up the points Arthur brought up one by one. Regarding natural light, I wonder if Ed would speak about the use of light in the Fort Lauderdale Museum? You have designed one gallery, at the IBM Building in New York, that has no problems with natural light because it's in a basement. But when you go into this gallery you *feel* you're going into a basement.

Barnes: The Dallas Museum has a temporary gallery for traveling shows where there is no natural light, probably for the very reasons Arthur Drexler brought up. Around the other galleries in the Dallas Museum are scoop skylights with automatic shades. They can be opened or closed, depending on how the museum wants to use them. The Fort Lauderdale Museum has very little daylight. It has one skylight that casts some light on the curved wall.

Obviously there are certain things—objects, sculptures, and so on—that are wonderful in light. If you talk to artists, and to the general public, you'll often find they like daylight in museums. Still, Arthur has a point. It is true that in the case of works on paper natural light is an absolute no-no. In the old days you could show sketches and paintings in the same galleries, and these days you can't. Paintings are shown at very high light levels, while works on paper are shown practically in candlelight. This presents quite an obstacle. Enormous adjustments have to be made to exhibit an artist's work in a way that will show the connections between sketches and paintings, for instance. The question of light value is a very hot issue.

Holzman: I think you'll probably agree that there is no one way to conserve paintings right now. In fact, there's a great conflict about how to conserve a work of art. We discussed problems of conservation and lighting levels very thoroughly at the Virginia Museum. We prefer natural light because it represents the full color spectrum and because it changes: if you're going to look at art more than once, it really provides the widest range. Certain galleries in the Virginia Museum, such as the ones for drawings, have no natural light whatsoever. Generally, however, there are four ways in which natural light comes into the building, depending on the circumstance: traditional gallery top lighting, one-sided louvered skylights, solar-glazed windows, and ceramic frit glass stair enclosures.

Moderator: Norman, you explained that you would use ultraviolet filters and louvered shades for the glass-block walls at LACMA. Do these still present problems in terms of lighting levels?

Pfeiffer: Each institution and each program has to be examined separately when it comes to the issue of natural versus artificial light. LACMA subscribes to the notion that there is no either/or in this business. It's good to have some galleries in which natural light is

58

available, and some in which no natural light is allowed. Because of the constricted site for this museum, we were forced to pile three floors of galleries together, thus preventing any natural light from coming through the ceiling of two of the floors. But since there is a tremendous amount of sunshine in Los Angeles, it seemed sinful not to admit some of this radiance into the building. Glass block has therefore been used as a skylight, but a skylight turned on its side. In a traditional museum skylight there are two and sometimes three layers of glass, shades, and louvers—sometimes including louvers that are mechanically adjustable to vary the intensity of the light. The method we used is different. The "skylight" and exterior wall are compressed into one: one face of the glass block is the outer layer; the ultraviolet filter, the middle layer; and a metal louver that diffuses light, the inner layer. Galleries enclosed by glass block are reserved primarily for the display of three-dimensional objects. These galleries are about 20 feet tall, and the louver of the glass block starts about 12 feet off the floor so that wall space is still available for hanging art.

Barnes: If you look at the "Water Lilies" in the Scaife Gallery at the Carnegie Museum of Art in Pittsburgh on a partly cloudy day, the light coming through the skylight is sometimes yellow, sometimes grayish, and the light intensity pulses up and down. The blues in the canvas come forward and recede and then the reds come forward. When I saw the "Water Lilies" on such a day I had the distinct feeling that Monet would have liked that exact variation and vibrancy of effect that was brought on by the uncontrolled natural light.

Moderator: Ed, would you speak about the curved wall at the Fort Lauderdale Museum in terms of installation? A curved wall is considered a bit undesirable for looking at paintings, especially head-on, for there is distortion, I believe.

Barnes: In the Fort Lauderdale Museum the curve is extremely gradual—a long, slow curve—and the other wall is a rectangle. There are two points of view about this issue. On the one hand is the classical position that the art must actually be framed by two columns, two pilasters, a cornice, and a baseboard, and that the architecture must engage with it in this way. On the other hand is the point of view that with certain kinds of paintings, such as Abstract Expressionist works that depend more on peripheral vision, the architectural frame is not as important as having the painting seem to float against a dematerialized wall surface. I'm not arguing for that solution as the only way to hang art, but I think it is interesting for some kinds of art to have a soft wall, or at least a wall that joins the ceiling to create a kind of light box.

In boxlike rooms with central doors like the rooms in most European museums, the entrances and exits of the galleries are lined up in a file. This has a strong

27

28

29

27.
Hugh Hardy.
28.
Malcolm Holzman.
29.
Paul Goldberger and Arthur Drexler.

architectural effect, but I would question whether this arrangement preempts some important places to hang pictures.

Moderator: The Dallas Museum has been criticized because of a loss of orientation that occurs as you waft through the series of spaces—whether roomlike or loftlike.[6] You are not constantly referred back to the long, linear spine by which you have entered.

Barnes: Dallas is unusual because you have a barrel-vaulted gallery meeting with a cross-axial spine to create a kind of constant movement in and out, in and out. Then you move from that space and, as you say, waft along. I don't think there's a right or a wrong way, but many different ways to handle it.

Holzman: At the Virginia Museum we have a foot in two buckets. Each collection is displayed in a series of very small formal rooms, some with large paintings and some with small ones. Each also has one extraordinary room: on the Mellon side is a rectangular one; on the Lewis side is a larger, double-height room, almost cubic in shape, with movable partitions. You can place artworks in the galleries that are appropriate to what you're showing and how you wish to display it. It's nice to have both types of rooms because it gives the curators and installation designers flexibility.

Moderator: Does that mean you should have large, flexible spaces for large-scale paintings and small, well-defined rooms for small-scale works?

Holzman: I don't think you can make rules about what art objects should be put in what rooms—that is, small art in small rooms and big art in big rooms, and no mixing of the two. It depends on how it's done.

Moderator: Norman, do you have any particular comments about how you plan to organize the spaces in the Los Angeles County Museum?

Pfeiffer: It may sound like we are copping out because we don't say it should be done this way or that. But in an institution where there must be a quarter of a million square feet of gallery space, clearly there needs to be more than one way to do these things, whether we are talking about light, the size of the gallery, circulation through the gallery, or the installation of the artworks.

The galleries in the Los Angeles County Museum have many variations. Even the new wing's top floor has a very traditional, almost Beaux-Arts organization of a series of boxlike rooms strung like a necklace; you walk right down the center and look at paintings on either side. On that level the artworks on display are smaller, traditional paintings done before the 1940s. The most permanent portion of the museum's collection will be located there, so flexibility is not a major priority. The

30

30.
Left to right: Edward Larrabee Barnes, Suzanne Stephens, Malcolm Holzman, Norman Pfeiffer, Hugh Hardy.
31.
Norman Pfeiffer.
32.
Edward Larrabee Barnes.

31

32

60

middle galleries are less fixed. This floor can become either a very traditional permanent space with a clear axis, or a more free-form space. About half of the walls are permanently in place, while the others are freestanding and can be configured to provide a more Miesian type of open space. The ground floor needs to offer flexibility for any conceivable kind of exhibition: one exhibition may use the whole space, for example, or two or three exhibitions could be shown simultaneously. Here there are basically no walls except those that separate the glass-block galleries from the main portion.

Moderator: Malcolm, you recently said in an interview that even spaces that lack architectural details—spaces without color or pattern or texture on the walls and floor—still make a statement.[7] For example, the Walker Art Center that Ed Barnes designed has all-white, detail-less rectangular volumes for gallery spaces, but they're not anonymous at all. It's really a strong museum statement.

Holzman: In the interview I was asked about anonymous or nondescript spaces to house art. I cited the Walker because it's one of the landmarks of modern museum design. Because the floor is white, the ceiling is white, the walls are white—everything is white—some people call it neutral. In fact it is one of the strongest kinds of space to exhibit art in. You have to deal with it, I think, rather aggressively, as the staff at the Walker generally does. I have yet to be in a space that's neutral. All spaces come with certain qualities. What architects try to do is to build into those spaces the qualities that we like to see, so that the art looks better.

Moderator: Brian O'Doherty wrote in the late seventies that we have reached a point where what we see first in the white box is not the art but the *space*.[8] The ideal gallery, he says, removes all elements that interfere with the perception that this is art. But don't you really want to add some moldings, window trim, portals, and columns?

Barnes: I don't have any desire to add moldings—I'm a great admirer of calm. I have talked to the directors of galleries about what it's like to have the structural concrete columns expressed regularly throughout the building, what it does to an exhibition organized in a linear fashion. It means that things have to fit into stanzas and verses. That's the trade-off. If you want to have a room with corners, you gain and you lose. I like the stability, the feeling of strength, the sense that the paintings are not hung against an amorphous space, but I personally don't see a reason to add a lot of molding and detail. I'm very interested in seeing what Michael Graves is going to come up with at the Whitney. If it's built, we'll all have a chance to see how art looks in that kind of heavily detailed architectural space, with central doors from one room to the next and all the rest of it.

Question from the Audience: I wonder if the architects take into consideration the fact that one doesn't go through a museum in one complete movement. There are times when you'd like to sit and look at a painting or rest for awhile.

Pfeiffer: I'd like to comment on that. It's an extremely important point. If you ask a curator what the ideal gallery experience is, you will get one set of answers. Mr. Drexler's point about the social role museums play today is well taken: the degree to which these institutions can satisfy the public determines their ultimate success. People go to museums today not only to look at the works of art, but to come together with other people. This is true also of theaters, in which the lobbies have become great social spaces. In the next decade public libraries will be serving a similar function. At the New York Public Library you may soon be able to buy a T-shirt, eat, schmooze, and take part in other activities.

Many things go into the design of a museum. For the average person it is very fatiguing to go to a museum, often because circulation is not clear. Once visitors enter a building, they barely know where they are in relation to the outside world. As you point out, there is no place to get out of the path and out of the experience of looking. Each museum addresses that problem in its own way. In our museums we have created specific areas where you can rest. And in LACMA, for instance, there are windows at the end of an axis so that all of a sudden you can see Wilshire Boulevard and regain a sense of orientation. All of these things affect how you feel in a building. Of course, the art has to be impeccably displayed, cared for, and lighted, but the patron is an equal part of the equation.

Notes

1.
Edward Tilton (1861–1933), in association with William Boring (1859–1937), won the competition to design the United States Immigration Station on Ellis Island in 1898. After Boring retired in 1915, Tilton worked on his own and then with Alfred Githens on the Asa Griggs Candler Library at Emory University in Atlanta (1926) and the Currier Gallery of Art in Manchester, New Hampshire (1929).

2.
Hardy Holzman Pfeiffer Associates had previously designed the headquarters for Best Products, a firm founded by Sydney Lewis that is located outside Richmond, Virginia. The partner-in-charge of the project was Malcolm Holzman. For more details see "Best Bets," *Progressive Architecture*, February 1981, pp. 66–73.

3.
John Peebles (1876–1934) and Finley Ferguson (1875–1936) of Norfolk, Virginia, designed a number of churches and hotels in the area.

4.
William L. Pereira (1909–1985) is known for the many schools, libraries, and office buildings he designed throughout southern California, as well as for the very noticeable Transamerica Tower he built in San Francisco in 1972.

5.
According to the *New York Times*, 6 February 1969, p. 32, the Museum of Modern Art was conducting a feasibility study to explore the possibility of either moving or building a tower over 23 West 53rd Street. The museum was also considering a proposal to enlarge its galleries by "tunneling under the sculpture garden behind the main building." Enclosing the garden may well have been seriously, if not publicly, debated.

6.
See Peter Papademetriou, "Dallas Museum of Art: Extending the Modernist Tradition of E. L. Barnes," *Texas Architect*, January–February 1985, pp. 36–51. Papademetriou notes that "while the circulation spine is the dominant organizing idea and constant reference for users of the museum, one might also argue that its intended clarity is obscured." Although the spine provides the main organizing principle, he goes on to say, it is the barrel-vaulted roof of the Contemporary Gallery that serves as the primary image of the museum from the outside, which only confuses understanding of the linear hallway. "In contrast to the bold, clear purity of the barrel vault, the spine is visually broken into segments by virtue of its sloped, ramped floor plane, and intervening changes in ceiling level. While this configuration has the...virtue of mitigating against a perception of its length, it causes a loss of intensity as well."
Papademetriou goes on to argue: "While the goals of the design—to promote a circulation pattern that minimizes the perceived distance traveled—are met in the arrangement, it is also true that a degree of disorientation results. Furthermore, without a visual reference between the galleries and the principal spine, the impression of one's position within the spatial progression is not sustained" (p. 46).

7.
Malcolm Holzman made this statement in an interview released by the Virginia Museum of Fine Arts at the time of the opening of the new West Wing in the fall of 1985.

8.
See Brian O'Doherty, "Inside the White Cube: Notes on the Gallery Space," Part 1, *Artforum*, March 1976, pp. 24–30. In this article O'Doherty argues that "the history of modernism is intimately framed by that [gallery] space. Or rather the history of modern art can be correlated with changes in that space and in the way we see it....The ideal gallery subtracts from the artwork all cues that interfere with the fact that it is 'art'....The outside world must not come in, so windows are usually sealed off. Walls are painted white. The ceiling becomes the source of light. The wooden floor is polished so that you click along clinically or carpeted so that you pad soundlessly, resting the feet while the eyes have at the wall....Unshadowed, white, clean, artificial, the space is devoted to the technology of esthetics" (pp. 24–25).

Michael Graves
Architect with a practice in Princeton, New Jersey. He has designed the Union County Nature and Science Museum and the projected plan for the Newark Museum.

Charles Gwathmey
Architect and principal of the New York firm Gwathmey Siegel & Associates Architects.

Rafael Moneo
Architect and educator. He has practiced and taught in Madrid and Barcelona and is currently chairman of the Department of Architecture in the Graduate School of Design at Harvard University.

Alan Plattus
Member of the faculty of the School of Architecture at Yale University. Until recently he was a professor of architecture at Princeton University.

Art and the Walls Without

Issues of expansion and growth in the urban context
December 12, 1985

National Museum of Roman Art
Rafael Moneo

Solomon R. Guggenheim Museum
Charles Gwathmey

Museum of Art and Archaeology, Emory University
Whitney Museum of American Art
Michael Graves

Response
Alan Plattus

Discussion
Suzanne Stephens, moderator

The National Museum of Roman Art
Rafael Moneo

I should first discuss the context of this particular museum, the National Museum of Roman Art in Mérida, Spain, because it differs from that of some of the other museums being considered in this series. Mérida is an old Roman city that was founded in 25 B.C. and became the most important Roman city in Spain. It was almost destroyed during the Arab invasion in the early eighth century, but it recovered very slowly until it became a rural center. The museum is located on the site of excavations begun in the late nineteenth century. Remains include a piece of the aqueduct that brought water to the town, the Roman road, and houses, including more recent ones dating from the Renaissance.

The museum's collection of over 30,000 pieces was assembled by José Alvarez y Saenz de Buruaga, who had worked there for about fifty years as archaeologist, chief curator, and then director of the museum. He finally convinced politicians of the need to create a new museum, particularly since new pieces are continually appearing that give an impressively strong idea of Roman culture in this remote town of rural Spain.

The major problem for me and for the archaeologists was how to deal with the ruins themselves. The street leading to the big monuments was crumbling, and we needed somehow to build a kind of retaining wall. Otherwise the excavations by the archaeologists would have been put in danger by the weight of traffic on the roads outside.

From the very beginning I had two ideas in mind: One was that the building should have its own presence; the other was that it should allude to this humble city's Roman traditions, which had been lost and completely ignored.

I don't know exactly how we came to the idea of a series of parallel walls hollowed to allow the formation of a navelike space, but probably it occurred to us because of the need for retaining walls. We realized we could solve the problem of the crumbling road through the design of this wall system. The walls also gave us a formidable amount of space to display the main pieces, such as the mosaics. They could be mounted on large, secondary brick cross walls as you might see in a library or archive.

The other problem that we had was linked with the change in levels of the site. On the lowest floor we created huge crypts as the setting for the existing "buried city." This museum is very explicitly trying to establish a connection to both the present city of Mérida and the past city that has been lost. The works of art exhibited in the museum will link it integrally to Mérida's past so that the place has a character and identity. The museum should be viewed in terms of its role of recapturing the lost quality of the Roman city and its urban condition.

66

1

2

4

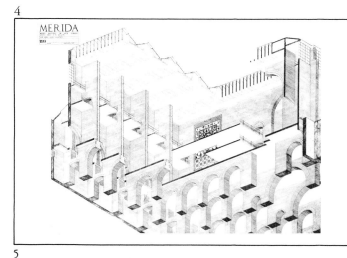

3

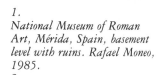

5

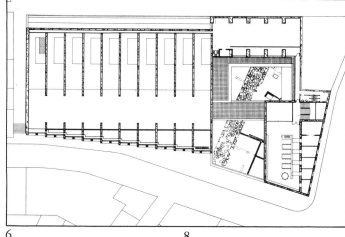

6

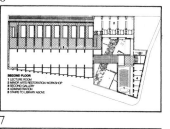

8

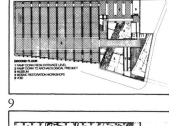

7

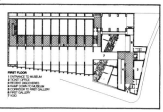

9

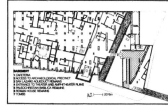

1.
*National Museum of Roman
Art, Mérida, Spain, basement
level with ruins. Rafael Moneo,
1985.*
2.
*National Museum of Roman
Art. View towards entrance.*
3.
*National Museum of Roman
Art. Central nave from ground
floor.*
4.
*National Museum of Roman
Art. Cut-away isometric,
worm's-eye view.*
5.
*National Museum of Roman
Art. Library plan.*
6.
*National Museum of Roman
Art. Second floor plan.*
7.
*National Museum of Roman
Art. First floor plan.*
8.
*National Museum of Roman
Art. Ground floor plan.*
9.
*National Museum of Roman
Art. Basement plan.*

The plan itself is rather simple. The administration
block, with offices for the curators, directors, and so
on, is separate and has its own entrance from the
street. Visitors coming into the museum enter on the
main floor. The ruins, including the theater and
amphitheater ruins and the remains of the aqueduct,
are in a basement level below the main floor and can be
entered from the outside. The ruins can also be reached
by a ramp from the main-floor space, where the central
nave of large arches is located. On the main floor, the
tall arches are carved out of the cross walls, which in
turn create narrow transverse galleries. On one side of
the nave are high windows that admit natural light; on
the other side, openings in each of the floors above

create bridges in the upper galleries that run through low-arched openings in the transverse cross walls. These gangplanks are in two galleries on the first and second levels above the nave level. They allow one to look down into the central nave and see large works of art, such as mosaics mounted on walls and statues installed in cryptlike niches. Small objects are displayed in artificially lit brass cabinets.

From the beginning I considered natural light to be the best source of illumination for this Roman city. The durability of the works of art, and of the place, makes this sort of light the most appropriate. Natural light is admitted through skylights and then bounces off the walls and permeates the lower floors through the large openings or light shafts in the various levels. Large side windows provide tangential illumination even in the basement, which is not open to the floors above. Everywhere there is a warm glow of natural light.

The question of preserving the ruins brought me to the idea of building the museum in the Roman manner; we wanted to establish a sense of natural contact with the ruins. Therefore we tried to keep the sense of scale, as well as the sense of the method of building. The building's construction is crucial in expressing the concern with preservation that was implicit in the whole concept of the museum. For instance, the use of brick that is not plastered over and has a minimal joint is one attempt to make a link with construction methods of the past. The brick walls are filled with unreinforced concrete—except for the walls in the main floor, which need steel reinforcement for stability. Reinforced concrete gangplanks with steel railings are slung between the walls above.

The wall alludes to Roman construction, but in the end it isn't as literal as it seems: it is much more an abstract support for the objects the museum contains. Some archaeologists might argue that we have been treating the ruins too casually or freely. To tell you the truth, the ruins are not so splendid, but they are quite valuable for understanding the nature of the city as well as Roman culture itself—and for understanding the kinds of spaces generated by the culture.

The architecture is intended to be a simple statement that becomes more complex as you look at the more concrete nuances. As you go through the museum, you suspect there is always more beyond what you see in the immediate situation. The alignment of the walls and the architectural spaces creates this sense. Sometimes we open the system of walls up to make a larger exhibition space, as required by the program. Many of the pieces are placed on the wall or on pedestals, but we are not going to display all the mosaics, since the director wants to avoid a feeling of overcrowding or of overwhelming the space itself.

11

10.
National Museum of Roman Art. Central nave from ground floor.
11.
National Museum of Roman Art. Main nave.

The National Museum of Roman Art
Mérida, Spain
Architect: Rafael Moneo.
Program: A 124,000-square-foot museum over an existing archaeological site, including exhibition space, restoration workshops, library, and offices.
Structure and materials: Brick bearing wall with concrete core wall and concrete slabs; granite flooring; ceramic tile roofs.
Cost: Approximately $3.25 million.
Consultants: Francisco Gonzalez Peiro and Rafael Luque, quantity surveyors; Jesus Jimeniz, Alfonso Garcia Pozuelo, structural engineers.

The Solomon R. Guggenheim Museum
Charles Gwathmey

What I'd like to suggest is that you accept the fact that the Guggenheim Museum needs to expand. This is not debatable from my point of view. It's clearly not debatable from the museum's point of view, and Thomas Messer, the director, is in the audience tonight if there are any questions about the need for expansion.

Our addition, when and if completed, will expand the space for exhibiting the permanent collection from about 7,000 square feet, which it has now, to 14,450 square feet. We would more than double the permanent exhibition space, in addition to using the full amount of space in the spiral for temporary exhibitions.

One of our concerns in this addition is to reveal all sorts of primary spatial conditions implicit in the original building, which we happen to think are phenomenal. The addition provides space for storage, conservation, staff offices, and a board room, so the entire Wright-designed building—both large and small rotundas—will be open as exhibition spaces.

I would like to go through the analysis that ultimately determined how we got to this scheme. It has always been critical that the large rotunda be consistently maintained as the image—the primary object—as that part of the composition that holds its own in this context. It has sky behind it, because of the lower adjacent buildings on 88th Street. No matter where you are standing—looking from the north, the south or from across the park—the large rotunda is the dominant fact of this composition. The interior of the large rotunda has been used quite successfully as a temporary exhibition space.

The small rotunda, on the north corner of the block between 88th and 89th Streets, has always been problematic in its relationship to the apartment building at 4 East 89th Street and to the original alley between the two buildings. The large and small rotundas are held together literally and formally by a horizontal band that anchors the two very different-sized elements to each other. The second floor of this rectilinear band is devoted to the Thannhauser collection, with offices occupying the third and fourth floors. On top of this section is a small rotunda holding the board room, which, being a crescent-shaped room, is a less than successful space.

An article in *Architectural Forum* of 1952 clearly shows the design of the first proposed addition, one envisioned by Frank Lloyd Wright.[1] The scheme shows the potential expansion of the museum, and presents a background piece, orthogonally gridded, that would anchor the small rotunda to the cityscape. Some historians insist that Wright's proposed annex was on the adjacent site, that is, the site of 4 East 89th Street. That is not true. In Wright's proposal, a 15-story slab 25 feet wide and about 90 feet deep contained artists' studios. They occupied approximately 12-

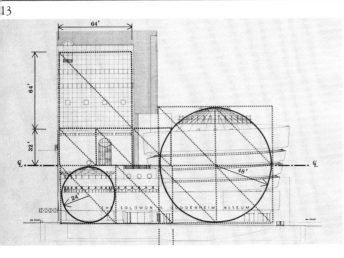

12.
*Solomon R. Guggenheim
Museum, New York, model of
proposed addition. Gwathmey
Siegel & Associates, Architects,
1985.*
13.
*Solomon R. Guggenheim Museum
addition. Elevation analytic
study.*

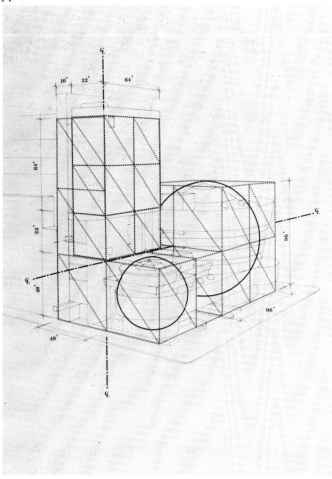

14.
*Solomon R. Guggenheim Museum
addition. Axonometric analytic
study.*
15.
*Solomon R. Guggenheim Museum
addition. Ground floor analytic
study.*

to 15-foot-deep spaces left free by placing the elevator core at the back wall. Clearly this is not adequate for additional exhibition space and/or other functions that need to be accommodated.

The deceptive thing about the drawing is that this studio building actually intersects the museum's existing fire stair behind the rotunda, and it is located on the present annex site. While the drawing makes it seem as if the slab slides behind the large rotunda, this is physically impossible in terms of both the plan and the site. If this scheme had been realized as we see it drawn, the slab would have intersected the large rotunda in a way that would have been difficult. Less difficult for Wright, very difficult for us.

The existing annex was designed by William Wesley Peters of Taliesin Associated Architects in 1968. The alley was still kept as a service corridor, while the second and third floors, totally separated from the existing building, were used for art storage. The fourth floor, which does connect to the main building, is called the Modern Masters Gallery and functions as an extension of the permanent collection located in the Thannhauser wing. By all accounts, this annex neither relates to the street and the buildings on East 89th Street nor makes a very successful transition to the original Frank Lloyd Wright building. It does not have a mediating materiality, a mediating scale, or a mediating geometry. It is, unfortunately, its own piece, self-contained and somewhat forbidding. However, it was built and designed so that the foundations and the columns can support six additional floors, something very important in our proposal.

The Guggenheim Museum was initially decried as an outrageous proposition in New York City—it was "out of context." Twenty-five years later this organic whole is loved (although the William Wesley Peters annex is criticized by some). Twenty-five years from now, I hope the same thing happens to us.

I think an analysis done by Jacob Alspector, the associate in our office who has been working intimately with us on this project, is very revealing. This geometric analysis shows that the large rotunda is basically a 96-foot-diameter circle inscribed in a 96-foot square, which is the primary site; the smaller rotunda is 48 feet in diameter, or half that. The heights of both rotundas are the same as their diameters. Overlaid on the rotundas are two squares of 96 feet, with the entry to the museum located where the two squares overlap. The large 96-foot squares break down into a four-foot-square orthogonal grid that is relentlessly extended through the building; the organic design is structured by an orthogonal grid that matches the city street grid. This was quite a discovery.

When you flip the plan and make it an elevation, you see that the same 96-foot-diameter circle inscribes the

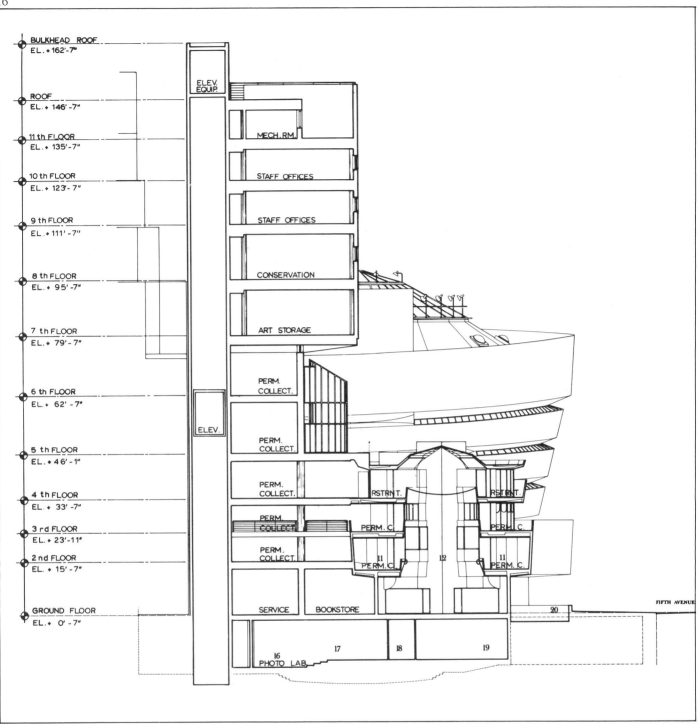

BULKHEAD ROOF
EL. + 162'-7"

ROOF
EL. + 146'-7"

11th FLOOR
EL. + 135'-7"

10th FLOOR
EL. + 123'-7"

9th FLOOR
EL. + 111'-7"

8th FLOOR
EL. + 95'-7"

7th FLOOR
EL. + 79'-7"

6th FLOOR
EL. + 62'-7"

5th FLOOR
EL. + 46'-1"

4th FLOOR
EL. + 33'-7"

3rd FLOOR
EL. + 23'-11"

2nd FLOOR
EL. + 15'-7"

GROUND FLOOR
EL. + 0'-7"

ELEV. EQUIP.

MECH. RM.

STAFF OFFICES

STAFF OFFICES

CONSERVATION

ART STORAGE

PERM. COLLECT.

PERM. COLLECT.

PERM. COLLECT.

PERM. COLLECT.

PERM. COLLECT.

ELEV.

SERVICE

BOOKSTORE

RSTRNT.

RSTRNT.

PERM. C.

PERM. C.

PERM. C.

PERM. C.

FIFTH AVENUE

PHOTO LAB.

16

17

18

19

20

11

12

11

16.
Solomon R. Guggenheim Museum
addition. Section.

Solomon R. Guggenheim Museum
New York, New York
Architect: Gwathmey Siegel & Associates Architects; Charles Gwathmey, Robert Siegel, partners-in-charge; Jacob Alspector, associate-in-charge.
Program: An eleven-story block comprising 28,935 square feet (new construction) and 5,637 square feet (renovation of annex) for gallery and support space. In addition, renovation of 4,790 square feet for galleries in existing Wright-designed museum.

Structure and materials:
Cream and terra cotta concrete, beige quarry tile, gray-green porcelain tiles, on a steel frame.
Cost: $10 million, estimated.
Consultants: Severud-Szegezdy Consulting Engineers, structural; John Altieri, P.E., mechanical.

17
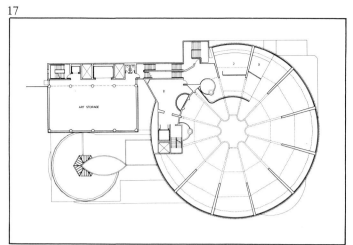

20
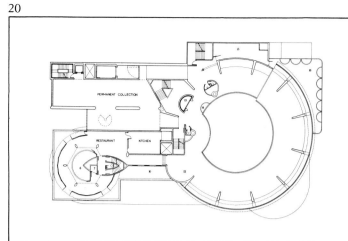

18
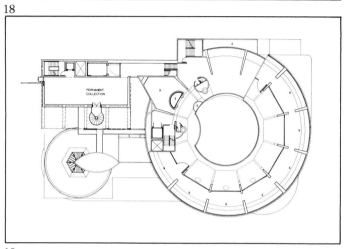

21
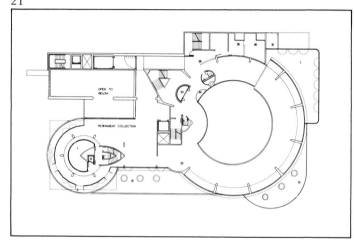

19
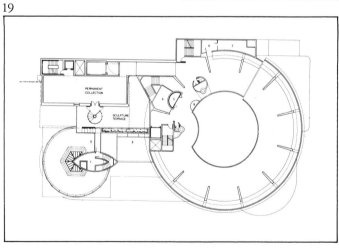

22
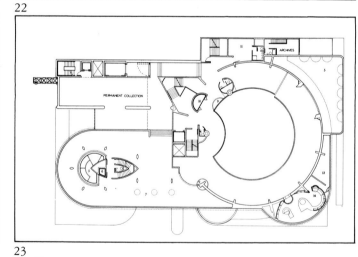

23
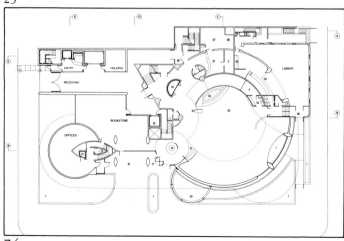

17.
Solomon R. Guggenheim Museum addition. Seventh floor plan.
18.
Solomon R. Guggenheim Museum addition. Sixth floor plan.
19.
Solomon R. Guggenheim Museum addition. Fifth floor plan.
20.
Solomon R. Guggenheim Museum addition. Fourth floor plan.
21.
Solomon R. Guggenheim Museum addition. Third floor plan.

22.
Solomon R. Guggenheim Museum addition. Second floor plan.
23.
Solomon R. Guggenheim Museum addition. Ground floor plan.

elevation of the large rotunda, and the 48-foot circle inscribes the elevation of the small one. If you extend that square up diagonally you see outlined the silhouette of Wright's original slab building.

Compositionally it is difficult to have a binuclear scheme where one element has a much stronger presence, mass, and scale than the other, and expect the two to hold together. This is why our proposal for this piece on this site is legitimate: in theory, we have tried to make a tripartite composition, thus helping the small rotunda establish its place in the context, while still allowing the large rotunda to appear as an independent element.

As you know, the Guggenheim is not a landmark building nor is it in a landmark neighborhood, as yet. Legally the museum could, if it so wanted, build an as-of-right structure that would be a massive street wall and make the museum an object in a room. That is one choice. The other choice would be to go to the building department and file an as-of-right proposal that would call for setting a stepped-back tower on top of the small rotunda, using it, if you will, as the hydraulic base lifting a tower above it. We did not want to do either scheme.

We began to investigate how to make a facade on 89th Street that not only defers to the street but turns the corner (on its own terms) and provides the appropriate backdrop for the small rotunda. The next issue was how to elaborate the addition. By cantilevering the top portion of our addition we can expand the building horizontally for extra space. It relates to the existing complex in the same geometric proportions because it uses the four-foot grid and the 96-foot height. After numerous studies in which we designed the top of the vertical element to be less figural and more abstract, we began to articulate the various parts, in a sense making a constructivist building. We see our design as establishing a dialogue with the fairly monochromatic, monolithic structure of the original museum. We decided to create a void between the top of the small rotunda and the underside of the cantilever, so that the rear wall is referential, a backdrop. Our cantilevered section thus becomes a third object floating in space. It is more static, however, because it is square.

As the plans show, for the first time there is total interconnection between the ramps of the large rotunda and the adjacent spaces. Now you will be able to go around every level of the large ramp, moving into the new galleries that pivot off this stair. The stair thus becomes an object in the space, not hidden by walls, and refers to the existing as well as the new organization. We also put the restaurant on the upper level of the small rotunda, where it will have access to those wonderful small balconies.

The new wing calls for removing everything in the existing wing except the actual floor slabs. On the lower floors—two to six—would be galleries that receive natural light from the north facade. The sculpture terrace of this new wing extends off the new fifth-floor gallery. You can come out onto this terrace and understand the building in a different light, perceiving not only the roofscape of the small rotunda but also the strong sculptural resolution of the large rotunda. You can look over the park while taking a break from viewing the art—something you couldn't do in the original museum.

The new sixth-floor gallery connects to the upper seventh-floor ramp of Wright's portion, which will now be open to the public (it is currently used for storage) and will be the final space for permanent exhibitions. Above are the open loft floors allowed by the transfer structure, which are totally flexible since circulation is contained in the core wall. Staff office floors are also located in the same type of space.

Our scheme as it presently exists shows a vertical reveal between the core wall and usable floors. The transfer truss is also articulated and slanted upward to act as a sort of ledge for the object. It is a cream color to match the existing color of the Wright building. The core wall is rendered in beige one-foot-square quarry tiles to refer to materials along 89th Street. The cantilevered element is faced subtly in gray-green slightly reflective tile cut on a four-foot grid. It alludes to the green of the park, while at times receding because it is slightly reflective. Underneath, the lower portion of the addition is constructed of poured concrete that is given a terra-cotta color.

The third element, a glass cylinder stair that connects the fifth and sixth floors, acts as a skylight for the fourth-floor permanent collection. It gives a sense of vertical continuity to the gallery space. These three skylights also set up a secondary interaction—a secondary trilogy—in comparison with the three major objects. For the first time, the ensemble holds itself in space in a tripartite framework. We think this resolution is dynamic as well as contextual.

The new object—28,935 square feet (gross) for offices, storage and galleries—will simultaneously coexist with and complete the composition. Yet it will allow the existing large rotunda to maintain its "objectness" and its presence—since this constitutes, after all, the identity of the Guggenheim Museum.

The Museum of Art and Archaeology at Emory University and the Whitney Museum of American Art

Michael Graves

The Museum of Art and Archaeology occupies a building we renovated at Emory University in Atlanta. The building was designed in 1916 by Henry Hornbostel, the wonderful Pittsburgh architect who built a lot of buildings at Carnegie-Mellon University, including the College of Fine Arts.[2] He designed the master plan for the buildings around the quadrangle at Emory. They are all clad in scraps of Georgian marble with slight variations in color; they look like a series of little palazzi marching down the quad.

We were given the task of renovating the inside and adding a couple of fire stairs. The two halves of the original building were different in section, so the building divided very neatly into the museum on one side and classrooms and offices for the departments of art history and anthropology on the other. The ground floor of the museum, which has its own special entrance off the lobby, is used for galleries displaying the permanent collection. From the rotunda at the entrance, a linear gallery leads to another round room at the end. On one side of this passage are small galleries and, on the other side, a large gallery for the Egyptian collection. On the second floor are two galleries for changing exhibitions: the gallery at the top of the narrow stairs is for drawings and special exhibitions; the other, larger gallery, used for a wider variety of exhibitions, is plainer and more flexible.

Since the museum's archaeological collection is more or less fixed, we wanted to embellish the building's interior in ways that would help you see the architecture of the cultures represented by each of the major collections. The Egyptian gallery, with its several mummy cases, has the plan of the temple of Ramses II stenciled on the floor. The stenciling, done by people in my office, takes an inexpensive wood floor and makes something special out of it. It also produces a scale that is contrasted with that of the plans stenciled in the Greek room, the pre-Columbian room, and the ancient Near-Eastern Room. Hornbostel's school of fine arts at Carnegie-Mellon has the plans of St. Peter's and other monuments inlaid in the marble floor.

The main galleries are lit by large gridded panels or laylights in the ceiling that resemble skylights and provide an overall luminosity to the rooms. Individual objects and vitrines are lit by spotlights mounted along the edges of the ceiling grids. The vitrines and other display cabinetry—made of birds-eye maple and ebony—are also lit internally.

Another museum project, yet to be completed, is the major renovation of the Newark Museum, a complex of four buildings with a rather good twenties building by Jarvis Hunt in the center. We've been working with Sam Miller, the director, and the museum trustees for about seventeen years on this and other parts of the museum. The project is out to bid, and presumably we'll start construction next month. The major work

76

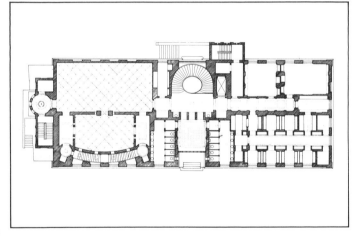

28

24.
Michael C. Carlos Hall, Emory University, Atlanta, Georgia. Henry Hornbostel, 1916–1919.
25.
Museum of Art and Archaeology, Michael C. Carlos Hall, Emory University, main gallery first floor. Michael Graves, Architect, 1985.
26.
Museum of Art and Archaeology. First floor plan, showing lobby, center; archaeology exhibition galleries, left; anthropology offices, right.

27.
Museum of Art and Archaeology. Side gallery, first floor.
28.
Museum of Art and Archaeology. Second floor plan, showing art exhibition galleries, left; art history offices, right.

Michael C. Carlos Hall, Emory University
Atlanta, Georgia
Architect: Michael Graves, Architect; Patrick Burke, Theodore Brown, project associates.
Program: A renovation of existing three-story 22,000-square-foot building for the university's Museum of Art and Archaeology, Department of Art History, and Department of Anthropology.

Structure and materials: Concrete block, steel framing, and stucco walls; marble, wood, and ceramic tile interior finishes.
Cost: $2.6 million.
Consultants: Jack Lynch & Associates, Inc., structural; Newcomb & Boyd Consulting Engineers, mechanical and electrical; Douglas Baker, lighting; David Scott, museum.

29.
*Whitney Museum of American
Art, New York, proposed addition. Michael Graves, Architect,
1985.*

involves renovating an old YWCA recently given to the museum for their children's activities and other educational programs, as well as designing new galleries and storage for the permanent collections, which will be housed in the main museum and the North Wing.

Then there is our proposal to add onto the Whitney Museum at 75th Street and Madison Avenue, completed by Marcel Breuer in 1966. Breuer's building is located on the southeast corner of 75th and Madison. Brownstones owned by the Whitney occupy the rest of the block south to 74th Street. As you know, New York blocks are 200 feet long, and if you look at the Whitney site plan, you will notice that the Breuer building occupies almost precisely half of the block. His concrete wall produces a break between the existing Whitney and the brownstones to the south. In 1966, when Breuer finished this building, we were of a different sensibility. At that time we did not like the brownstones as we do now. Breuer was quoted in *Newsweek* magazine saying that he thought the context was mediocre, and he therefore used the concrete walls to shut it out.[3]

Breuer's building steps from the lower level—set back about 30 feet from the "street wall"—forward to the top. It is designed to offer a sense of marvelous monumentality on a large scale that is played against a small-scale entrance canopy. In establishing design guidelines for a new building on the rest of the site, the city now requires that buildings come out to the edge of the sidewalk to create a uniform street wall. If Breuer were building his museum today, he would have to make the street facade a sheer plane rather than go with the current stepped facade. So it is no longer possible to think of Breuer's building as a segment of a whole that could simply be continued down the block.

In Breuer's scheme, there are approximately 60,000 square feet above ground and about 20,000 square feet underground, for a total of roughly 80,000 square feet. The Whitney expansion program calls for about 130,000 square feet. If we followed the setbacks required above the height of Breuer's building, we would find certain problems with the massing.

Other recent museums, like Ed Barnes' Dallas Museum or Richard Meier's High Museum in Atlanta, have generous sites. In orienting these buildings, in establishing a legible center and an understandable sequence of museum spaces inside, the architects were not dealing with the kinds of controls we have on very tight sites such as ours or the Guggenheim's. Like Gwathmey Siegel's proposed addition to the Guggenheim, we are making a vertical building.

Because the Whitney expansion will occupy the rest of the block south to 74th Street, Breuer's concrete wall, placed approximately at the halfway point, acts as the central dividing element in a kind of diptych. In

Whitney Museum of American Art
New York, New York
Architect: Michael Graves, Architect; Karen Wheeler Nichols, Theodore Brown, Robert Marino, John Diebboll, project associates.
Program: A major extension of approximately 134,000 square feet and renovation of existing building to create approximately 40,000 square feet of new gallery space, plus office space, theater, restaurant, expanded study facilities, and commercial retail space.
Structure and materials: Gray-pink granite on a steel frame.
Cost: $37.5 million, estimated.
Consultants: Not provided by architect.

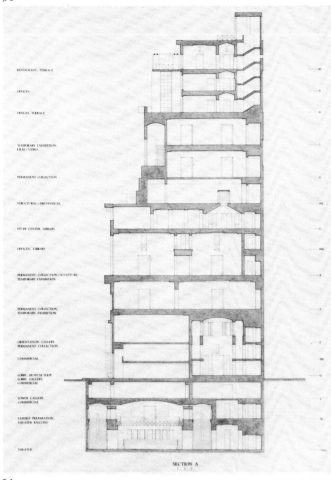

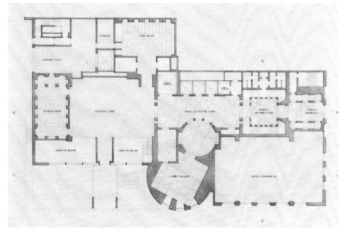

30.
*Whitney Museum of American
Art, addition. Transverse section.*
31.
*Whitney Museum of American
Art, addition. Ground floor
plan, showing lobby gallery, center; existing lobby, left; retail
space, right; along with
additional lobby and support
space. Due to revisions being
undertaken, additional plans were
unavailable for publication.*

paintings such as Renaissance annunciations, there are often columns dividing the pictorial space and separating the archangel on the exterior from the Virgin on the interior. The two parts of the painting interact formally across the line created by the column; the two figures are separated from each other and yet united by the message being conveyed. Rather than use a singular division such as a column, we have chosen a variant—the space or room, as seen in an annunciation painting by Piero della Francesca. In the Whitney, a cylinder, a kind of spatial hinge, is inserted between Breuer's half and our half, connecting the two and containing a series of spaces for functions special to the Whitney such as the lobby gallery, the orientation gallery, a display space for Calder's Circus, and so on. Inside, Breuer's large elevator has been reoriented so that the space between the two buildings becomes a hinge of circulation connecting the old and the new. On the first floor, we have added another door on 74th Street, which would be open primarily at night to give access to the lower floors and the auditorium.

We were commissioned basically to provide new exhibition space for the Whitney's permanent collection. Less than one percent of the collection is being shown now, and 40,000 square feet of new galleries will still only allow less than five percent of the art to be shown. So we'll still be denied seeing a lot of Edward Hoppers. The exhibition space on the second floor, which will incorporate both halves of the building, will display the permanent collection up to World War II. The rooms are arranged so that a visitor's path through them forms a kind of figure eight from the lobby in front of the elevators and Breuer's stair, through the galleries, and back. The third and fourth floors of Breuer's half will remain intact and will be used for temporary exhibitions; the presentation of the permanent collection will be continued in the new half.

The fifth floor is presently occupied by offices. We have installed the library and study center there because the ceiling is low and we want to keep the project as economical as possible. Throughout we are maintaining the same ceiling levels that presently exist. The sixth and seventh floors, above the present Breuer building, contain galleries for both the permanent collection and temporary exhibitions. A stair connects these two floors along the front edge of the building, behind a large eyebrow window that looks out to Madison Avenue. Finally, there are offices and a restaurant on top.

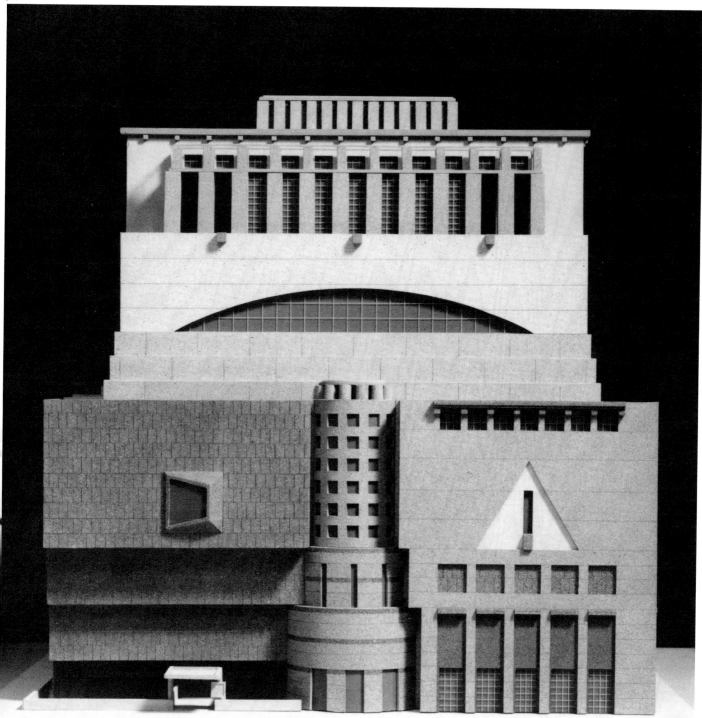

32.
Whitney Museum of American
Art, addition. Model.

Response
Alan Plattus

Having seen and heard about the three major projects off and on for some time now, I am emboldened to say that each of them in its peculiar way, and all of them collectively, make me quite optimistic about the future of the museum as an urban institution. This optimism must be placed in the context of several decades of frenetic museum building. During this time, despite the architectural bravura of the designs and the journalistic hype with which they were received, much of the work seemed to oscillate between cultural anesthesia on the one hand and spatial titillation on the other—sometimes in the same project. In almost every case there is some attitude toward the "problem" of the museum that turns out to confirm all the old myths and clichés, as well as a few not so flattering new ones, such as the "museum as suburban shopping mall."

One myth that has survived and even flourished throughout a century of wildly divergent and apparently radical cultural critiques is that of the museum as an atemporal, acontextual monument. All three of these projects subject the monument to a reinsertion into urban space and, most importantly for the problem at hand, urban time. For Rafael Moneo's project, that time is the *longue durée* of archaeology. The museum stands as the index of a process of sedimentation that has produced almost inevitably something other than the allegedly neutral backdrop of so many museums. In the case of Charles Gwathmey's project, there is an explicit revision of the temporal expectations suggested by the Guggenheim, which Val Warke once described as waiting "conspicuously and impatiently for New York to be Broadacred."[4] Gwathmey's addition signals the fact that this has not and will not come to pass, and so asks us to reevaluate the relationship between a monumental institution and the city of which it must be part, and the way in which that institution may reintegrate itself into its context. Finally, in the case of Michael Graves' addition to—or recompletion of—the Whitney Museum, two versions of the "timeless monument" conspire to thrust each other back into the flow of urban time in a way that seems to me much more significant than the effect of either by itself.

What seems clear is that the challenging questions associated with all three of these projects arise as a result of specific circumstances that might be seen as constraining, or even nonnegotiable. Each of the architects has adopted a thoroughly opportunistic attitude toward these circumstances. Therefore, it seems fair to ask if, beyond the inventive strategies deployed, one can draw any more general lessons about the nature of the institutions in question. In fact, the archaeological strategy developed by Rafael Moneo's project might well serve as a more general metaphor for what is at stake here, which in all of the projects concerns the museum in relation to the historical process of city building. Only relatively recently have planners like Haussmann in Paris seen fit to extract monuments from their accreted context, tearing down, for example, the

82

buildings around Notre Dame, presumably so we could take better photographs of it. But the ideology of the isolated, inviolate monument is just that, an ideology that challenges the way cities had always developed, by the accretion, juxtaposition, absorption, and transformation of institutions and monuments. To suggest that the museum (and perhaps, by implication, its context) in the contemporary city must again be part of that process is obviously provocative. It may also be enormously refreshing.[5]

Discussion

Michael Graves
Charles Gwathmey
Rafael Moneo
Alan Plattus
Suzanne Stephens, Moderator

Moderator (Suzanne Stephens): Before taking up the larger urban issues, I would like to refer back to some of the criticisms that have been raised about the projects regarding the program and the growth and expansion of the museums, since these are particularly controversial points. Michael, critics have questioned your scheme, which more than doubles the size of the Whitney, and have pointed out that a lot of space in the addition—including the exhibition area for archives, the rare book room, the auditorium, and the restaurant, for example—is generated by the program. These critics have asked if such a program is really necessary for the Whitney.[6] Does the Whitney have to do all these things in order to be a "museum"? Wouldn't a smaller Whitney be architecturally better?

Graves: Today, as you know, education is such an important part of the museum experience that a museum needs an auditorium. It's hard to imagine a museum without a place for discussion of the work within it. Yes, it could be across the street. And so could your kitchen be across the street from your dining room. But it makes life a little tougher. Perhaps the issue gets more questionable when we talk about an expanded bookstore. But that's not very big. And, in perspective, the building isn't terribly big compared to the Met or the Museum of Modern Art.

I wonder if the question about size is a guise for the stylistic question that a lot of people raise about my design vis-à-vis Breuer's building. I think this is a moment in history where we have to realize that we're not just building *Kunsthallen* or picture galleries. We're building institutions that have places for discussion, places for study, and a social climate as well as a climate in which to see painting and sculpture. I'm all in favor of that. I'm bowled over, quite frankly, that the building is described as too large.

Any architect who builds a museum today—or who built one yesterday—has to understand that his building is going to be changed. The inside is going to be changed frequently, and the outside is probably going to be added to or subtracted from. We can look at the history not just of the Museum of Modern Art but also of the Met. It has gone through transformation after transformation. The constant change that institutions like this face is endemic. It's endemic to architecture. It's endemic to city-making, as Alan Plattus said.

Moderator: The Whitney has been criticized for being too bulky in the design of the top five floors above the Breuer building. In a very thoughtful article in *Artforum* magazine, Joseph Giovannini analyzed the building above the fifth floor in relation to the galleries provided on the seventh and eighth floors. He argued that because the seventh and eighth floors (which are called the sixth and seventh because you aren't counting the mechanical and structural transfer floor) each have about 5,000 square feet of exhibition space, you could

84

aise the roof on the existing fifth floor—where you have located offices and other support services—and insert the seventh- and eighth-floor galleries, and build a tower for administration over the south end.[7]

Graves: We were asked by the staff and the trustees if we could keep the building open during construction. If you take the fifth floor roof off, you must change the mechanical systems above it at that time and you must also remove all the painting and sculpture. Thus the building would have to close, like the Museum of Modern Art did.

On top of that, both our scheme and Giovannini's proposal would increase the size of the columns floor by floor. So the Whitney would have to close off part of the building on a floor-by-floor basis at least. It's not that we didn't think of the scheme that Giovannini suggested, but it seemed appropriate to keep the fifth-floor ceiling height at 8 feet 9 inches for the library and study center. The floors above that are as big as we can make them, given the setback requirements. And there you have it.

Moderator: Critics have also argued that your designing over and around the Breuer building has destroyed the integrity of the original building as a work of art. The argument is that because your building enters into the perceptual field, it changes the whole gestalt. As Hamilton Smith, who worked with Breuer on the Whitney, pointed out at a community board hearing not long ago, the Whitney is not like a scrap of newspaper that's used in a collage by Braque. Rather, it is like a complete painting, and it is now losing its "frame"—that is, the space around it—by being incorporated into a "radical collage."[8] There are some architects who say that, because of the program, you should have refused a job of this size.

Graves: Do you think *they* would have?

Moderator: I'm not an architect. What about the argument that you should leave the Breuer building, a culminating statement of his career, intact as an artwork, which means leaving the space around and above it a void?

Graves: Given that Breuer wanted to build a tower on top of Grand Central, we know that if he were alive today he would accept the Whitney commission.[9] We know that if Tom Armstrong, the director of the Whitney, had asked him to make a horizontal space, he would have.

I'm really tired of the assumption that he or others in this room wouldn't have designed a building spanning the present Whitney. I've done it. It is worth discussing. But the size of the building is quite okay. It's not inappropriate for that street. It's not inappropriate for that site. The problem, I think, with the original

33

34

35

33.
Frances Halsband and Charles Gwathmey.
34.
Audience, December 12, Thomas Messer at center right.
35.
Rafael Moneo.

85

building is that it was conceived by Marcel Breuer and his partner Hamilton Smith to stand alone. And whether or not the museum's concrete side walls have a knock-out panel for future expansion, Breuer knew that there would be an addition or at least the possibility of one, for it was discussed with him at one time.[10] We do not know what he said he would do. While it is superficially called a stylistic question, the issue about the difference between his age and ours is real. There was a different sensibility then. Even Wright's building for the Guggenheim struggles to stand alone. Breuer's does so less successfully because of its frontality and because of its street face. Wright's Guggenheim does not have that frontality. Therefore one could say that Breuer's is more of a city building than Wright's. Put in those terms, adding onto it—beside it and above it—is, I think, okay. I would do it again in a flash.

Moderator: Charles, Wright's 1952 project for the high-rise behind the Guggenheim that you showed us is a 15-story gridded rectangular slab that appears to have a low-relief, allover texture, much like a quilt. Because of its gray-green porcelain tile and that cantilevered section, your addition not only steps farther into the picture plane but is more actively composed, with more indentation and more articulation. Would you say that this composition would tend to dominate, or at least compete with, the rest of the composition, which includes Wright's two rotundas?

Gwathmey: Can Michael answer that question? I'd rather answer Michael's question because I could do it better.

Graves: From what's been written about you and me, I think we've probably got the wrong clients.

Gwathmey: I don't think it's aggressive to recompose what one may consider a discordant composition in the context. I do not necessarily mean a discordant composition as an object in space. But if we are dealing with context, then I think Alan's comment was terrific. Here one is allowed to reevaluate the compositional aspects of an "object" building and its context and to mediate between the two with a new addition.

I think what we have attempted to do is just that, without, however, imitating a tartan orthogonal grid. Our building is an orthogonal grid, a four-foot grid, subtle, if you will, but clearly an object in space that is suspended almost as if it were upside down. It acts as a kind of metaphor for the Guggenheim itself. That sort of tripartite composition—different from Michael's—was compelling for us, and it solved the program requirements.

Incidentally, in terms of criticism, negative or positive, these evenings at least allow us to present the facts and allow people to evaluate propositions that are based on the facts—leading, I hope, to some clearer criticism. But I would like to say something about the Breuer building, about why I think Michael's scheme is ingenious and also fair. It picks up on what Ulrich Franzen said about three months ago. The concrete shear wall in the middle of the Whitney block has within it the clear implication that it could be taken away and the extrusion could be continued, which I think could have been Breuer's intention.

The fact that the shear wall is there allows Michael to put a block to the south end. The stair forms a link around the shear wall. To build over the top, stepping back from the street, is actually compelling. The two remaining walls, the silhouette of the northeast corner, and the facade of the street are retained. In essence that is the Breuer object. It's not something that is viewed from above. It's not as three-dimensional as the Guggenheim in its volumetric presence. It is oriented to the street facade, and it seems extruded, as if sliced off by a machine, not a separate entity. The quality is retained, in its most positive sense, in the composition that Michael has offered us.

Moderator: Getting back to a very specific question about the Guggenheim, could you explain the intent behind your choice of colors and what they are supposed to do compositionally for the whole?

Gwathmey: The attempt in the color choice, and in the overall articulation of the parts, is to make an assemblage—a composition of pieces that is articulate in its own right. The assemblage becomes a constructivist-type object, a counterpoint to the existing building on its own terms; yet in each of its parts, it also refers to both the street and the existing buildings.

Graves: I think it's a very good move. I think it's brilliant and simple: the color of the park on one side and the very subtle gray-green on the other suspend the Wright building in a way that hasn't occurred before. In Wright's scheme the quilted backdrop was beige, but assuming that Wright saw his building as an extension of the park rather than an extension of the city, making the wall a subtle green is really a stroke of genius.

Moderator: Rafael, in the November 1985 issue of *Architectural Review*, there is a report that some people are unhappy about the Mérida museum in the way it intrudes on the neighboring streets. It is said that the museum, especially that tall, sheer west elevation, refuses to "condescend."[11]

Leon Krier has also criticized the building for looking like a system building, "a factory that is endless. It could continue to the left, to the right, in all directions," he says. "A public building in a small city should not really look like a factory if it is of cultural importance. It should look like a finite building that has an entrance."[12]

Moneo: I wanted to build something that recovered for the city the dimensions of Roman buildings. From the very beginning I realized that the bulk of the building wasn't going to relate to the existing houses. I accepted it as a given, and it was accepted by the people who were responsible for the museum itself. The idea of context in this case will work exactly in reverse. Our problem was really to dominate and to be more relevant than the houses around the museum. I also attempted from the very beginning to capture the sense of the Roman public works such as aqueducts, marketplaces, shipyards, and so on. It was naturally a personal view, but it was my view of Roman architecture. I wasn't dealing with the problem of the facade. In other projects, such as the Bankinter building I am doing now in Seville, the problem of the facade is the substantive one. But in the case of the museum, the facade was generated by the fabric itself. I think that the result is determined by the urban conditions of the building, the very humble grid on which the city is based. In paying attention to the grid, the museum provides an end to the endless fabric.

Moderator: I'd like to go back and pursue one issue we haven't really discussed tonight, although we have in the past two sessions: the issue of the roomlike gallery versus the loftlike exhibition space. Michael, in a recent interview you said that there are many ways a Georgian-style room can be arranged, but only one way a modern room can be arranged to look correct.[13]

Graves: I said there is probably a best way that a modern room can be arranged, whereas there are usually several ways that could be thought of as "best" in a Georgian room or another traditional room.

Moderator: You said that the National Gallery by John Russell Pope would look fantastic with modern paintings hanging in it because of the tension between the traditional architecture and the contemporary art.[14] How do you feel that tension would work?

Graves: The Whitney's permanent collection is more or less predictable. We generally know the character of the paintings that are going to be displayed in each of the rooms. Let me put the question back to you: Would it be appropriate to show, say, twelve Hoppers in the same kind of space that you would show twelve de Koonings? Probably not. The light is different in the paintings; the surfaces are dramatically different; the attention is different. Should the walls, the texture, the style, the size or shape of the room in which the works are displayed also be different?

I think the more pertinent question is: If an architect were creating a room for works by Edward Hopper, would he make it Hopper-like? Probably not. Hopper does it better. How would you do it, though? Would you have a white wall with a gray carpet or a white wall with a wooden floor? Would you try to create the

40.
Left to right: Rafael Moneo,
Suzanne Stephens, Michael
Graves, Charles Gwathmey.

room's proportions to relate to the pictures—those very intimate scenes? Wouldn't you do a de Kooning room quite differently? You would want to confront those great paintings in a room that would give them presence, give them their distance.

The Whitney encompasses the idea of a *Kunsthalle*, or changing gallery for temporary shows, as well as galleries for the permanent collection. At the Emory University museum, we had a mummy room packed full of stuff that we knew was not going to change for a very long time, but we also created very neutral galleries upstairs where shows are changed frequently. In fact, the director of that museum recently mounted a number of shows in the upper gallery. He has made little rooms; he has made walls; he has essentially done what other museums do.

Breuer's galleries, those big neutral volumes, will, by their grandness, allow that kind of temporary exhibition to continue. One of the things I know we will have a lot of discussions about with the staff when we build the Whitney—and we will build the Whitney—is the quality of light and detail in the rooms. I remember when the Stuttgart museum was under construction, Jim Stirling had a room built in a shed beside the museum to test different kinds of lighting, different colors of whites, creams, and grays for the walls, and different configurations for the doors. They could even try out paintings in there. Now the galleries work brilliantly because he gave them the kind of time and attention they needed.

But in the last twenty years or so, we have gone through a period in which it was thought that all walls in modern galleries had to be white, all ceilings had to be neutral, and all lighting had to come down from little cans—one of modern architecture's inventions.

Gwathmey: I agree with that absolutely. At the Guggenheim we have very different dimensional and spatial limitations than Michael has. But we will clearly attempt some minor elaborations in the interiors that will be provoked by decisions of the curators of that museum—what works they choose, and how they organize the exhibition and chronology of the permanent collection.

Notes

1.
Architectural Forum, April 1952, pp. 141–144. According to a statement by William Wesley Peters of the Frank Lloyd Wright Foundation on 12 September 1985, the 15-story studio building was originally proposed for a site at 4 East 89th Street, not the site of the proposed Gwathmey Siegel addition. Peters has submitted a drawing to support his case to the city.

2.
Henry Hornbostel (1867–1961), a graduate of the School of Mines at Columbia University, studied at the Ecole des Beaux-Arts in Paris. In 1904 he won a competition to design the Carnegie Institute of Technology in Pittsburgh, Pennsylvania, where he subsequently founded the school of architecture and was its first director. His firm, Palmer and Hornbostel, designed city halls in Oakland, California (1910), and Pittsburgh (1910) and school buildings on various campuses, including Emory University (1920).

3.
See "The New Whitney," *Newsweek*, 3 October 1966, pp. 98–100. The article quotes Breuer as saying, "Maybe I built it to rebel against skyscrapers and brownstones. I didn't try to fit the building to its neighbors because the neighboring buildings aren't any good" (p. 98).

4.
See Val K. Warke, "The Song of the Sirens: A Rhetoric of Urban Monumentality," *The Harvard Architecture Review* IV, "Monumentality and the City" (Spring 1984), pp. 123–47.

5.
Alan Plattus' essay "Friends (and Enemies) of the Museum," in *Design Book Review*, Summer 1985, pp. 20–25, is a discussion of several approaches to thinking about the proper setting for viewing art in museums. In his article, essentially a review of Helen Searing's *New American Art Museums* (New York: Whitney Museum of American Art, in association with University of California Press, Berkeley and Los Angeles, 1982) and of *Lotus International* 35 (1982), an issue on museum architecture, Plattus sees the enemies of the museum as those who "not only tolerate, but revel perversely in the dim illumination and musty atmosphere that is often the price of viewing an artifact in its 'original' context." "Friends" of the museum include the functionalists, who "weigh the value of an always ephemeral, and sometimes spurious, historical aura against the carefully calculated footcandles and controlled environment of the modern museum, adding for good measure points for public accessibility and didactic presentation" (p. 20).

6.
See Paul Goldberger's reassessment, "For the Whitney, Adding Less May Result in More," *New York Times*, 11 August 1985, sec. 2, p. 31, which followed his initial evaluation, "A Daring and Sensitive Design," *New York Times*, 22 May 1985, sec. C, p. 20. In the later article Goldberger asks, "Is this sweeping building program really necessary?...It is not impossible that a smaller, less ambitious Whitney could be a better one." For additional appraisals of the Whitney design, see Roger Kimball, "Michael Graves Tackles the Whitney," *Architectural Record*, October 1985, pp. 113–15; Hilton Kramer, "The Whitney's new Graves," *The New Criterion*, September 1985, pp. 1–3; Carter Wiseman, "Graves Questions at the Whitney," *New York*, 19 August 1985, pp. 74–78; Michael Sorkin, "Save the Whitney," *The Village Voice*, 25 June 1985, p. 104; Hamilton Smith, "Don't Ruin the Whitney," *New York Times*, 20 July 1985, sec. 1, p. 23; and Thomas Hoving, "My Eye, An Open-and-Shut Letter," *Connoisseur*, August 1985, p. 9. For a discussion of the controversy itself, see Suzanne Stephens, "A Confrontation in Context," *Manhattan, inc.*, January 1986, pp. 141–45.

7.
See Joseph Giovannini, "A Grave Situation for Marcel Breuer's Whitney," *Artforum*, November 1985, pp. 84–86. He writes: "The fifth floor has been allocated for offices and nongallery use, since the Breuer ceiling is too low (8 feet 9 inches) to be used as a gallery. The use of this fifth floor suggests a remarkably simple key to liberating the Breuer building from the temple—perhaps one of the other possible alternatives. Because the entire fifth floor is devoted to functions that could easily be put in a tower, all Graves has to do is switch floors, putting the 5,000-square-foot seventh- and eighth-floor galleries on the fifth floor, which is planned to offer about 14,850 square feet net. The seventh- and eighth-floor galleries would not only fit easily into the fifth floor, the Museum would also potentially gain nearly 5,000 square feet of gallery. The price to pay is simply the price of elevating the roof of Breuer's fifth floor several feet to a height acceptable for galleries.... The switch would not only give the museum about 10 percent more gallery space—and on five rather than six floors—but would consolidate the galleries within the first five floors of the building" (p. 86).

8.
These comments were made at a hearing of Community Planning Board 8 on 13 November 1985.

9.
In 1968 Marcel Breuer proposed erecting a 55-story tower on top of Grand Central Terminal, which had just been designated a landmark a few years earlier. Breuer's proposal was abandoned after a storm of protest. For a particularly spicy reaction, see Sybil Moholy-Nagy, "Hitler's Revenge," *Art in America*, September 1968, pp. 42–43.

10.
See Giovannini, "A Grave Situation," in which he notes that Tom Armstrong, director of the Whitney Museum, told a public gathering that Breuer had planned on future additions and had indicated the location for such additions by installing a punch-out wall on the south end of the building, where the elevators and stairs are placed.

11.
See Peter Buchanan, "Rafael's Spanish Romans," *The Architectural Review*, November 1985, pp. 38–47, in which the author observes: "The Museum has been criticised for its lack of contextual response, for the way its hugeness intrudes upon the neighbouring streets" (p. 46).

12.
Leon Krier, in *The Charlottes-ville Tapes* (New York: Rizzoli, 1985), p. 80. Although Krier says he finds the museum "absolutely adorable," he goes on to criticize it for having two different expressions for interior and exterior: "As you enter the building you have a large basilica space; outside you have the appearance of a system building."

13.
Sarah Williams, "Galleries for Tomorrow's Art," *Art News*, November 1984, pp. 9–10. Graves is quoted as saying, "There's only one way that furniture in the modern room looks right, and there are many ways that the Georgian room can be arranged" (p. 10).

14.
Ibid. Graves continues: "I think a great show of modern paintings could be hung in John Russell Pope's National Gallery in Washington, and the tension between the two would be fantastic. I also can imagine an exhibition of paintings in a modern space, with neutral walls and neutral ceilings and neutral floors. And for me, the architecture keeps getting in the way, because it's never neutral enough" (p. 10).

Conclusion
Suzanne Stephens

As a concluding statement, I would like to make a few observations about this series of discussions. While no unanimous opinion has been expressed on the specific direction museum design should take, we have discussed certain approaches that may be worth exploring. The manner in which the space that contains art is handled is considered very important: instead of the loftlike neutral modernist spaces favored in museum design of the last several decades, the traditional roomlike gallery is now highly regarded. At the same time, the panelists emphasize that this kind of space functions best when shaped for specific works of art. Galleries for temporary exhibitions or for artworks yet to be acquired (or executed) still make the flexible loftlike space tempting, if not always ideal.

Natural light is favored by a good many of our panelists due to the subtle and changing tonalities it casts on the art. However, the curatorial community represented here has expressed strong reservations about the use of natural light since it requires such complex technical precautions to prevent the art from being harmed. With regard to the use of artificial illumination, incandescent light ranks higher than fluorescent, judging from the examples cited. We didn't spend enough time on this distinction, I'm afraid. Be that as it may, a mixture of natural ambient light and direct incandescent light seems to be the most acceptable solution. Skylights and light monitors have been given as the best way to admit natural light, although there is some feeling that sidelighting—through windows or clerestories—has the added advantage of providing glimpses of the outside world to help orient the museumgoer. Other elements have been cited as mitigating museum fatigue, particularly the enfilade arrangement of galleries and/or the adjoining rotunda/atrium/outdoor court.

As for architectural elements that offer visual breaks from the study of artworks, aside from doors and windows, details such as moldings and cornices received particular mention. The balance between architecture and art is, of course, recognized as a quite delicate one. If there is too much "architecture," it overshadows the work on view. This has proved to be the case as much with modern museums, where pipes and ducts attract attention, as with traditional museums, where marble and moldings vie with the art.

Architectural features borrowed from different building types are considered detrimental to the art experience because they often carry very strong associations with the original type. Thus the panelists have objected to escalators because of the association with department stores. Galleries placed below ground have reminded panelists of less noble spaces. Then, too, while the museum is increasingly called upon to provide space for fundraising events, many panelists feel that areas set aside for gala parties contribute to the country-club atmosphere that seems to be taking over once hallowed halls.

The pressures on museums to expand their collections lead to larger museum spaces, larger staffs, higher budgets, more fundraising events, and so on. The impact on neighborhoods in which museum expansion is taking place is one issue we have addressed, although the outcome of two of the case studies presented has not been fully determined.[1] Whatever the case, how and why a museum should grow is an extremely sensitive and complicated question. Unfortunately, solutions do not come as easily as problems. But in helping to call attention to many of the considerations in museum design today, I hope we have contributed something to the architectural understanding of this complex array of issues.

1.
As this publication goes to press, the Whitney addition is being redesigned by Michael Graves. It is reported that the expansion has shrunk in size, but the updated sections, elevations, and plans for most of the gallery levels have not yet been released. As for the Guggenheim extension, Gwathmey Siegel presented a scheme to the Board of Standards and Appeals, the city agency that has final review powers, on 25 June 1986. A second hearing was held September 17, 1986, with final decision postponed. According to the New York City Landmarks Law the Guggenheim is not eligible for landmark status until 1989.